951
W

69-5471

CHINA:
THE ROOTS OF MADNESS

CHINA: THE
ROOTS OF MADNESS

A Documentary
　Written by Theodore H. White
　Produced by Mel Stuart

W · W · NORTON & COMPANY · INC · NEW YORK

Library of Congress Catalog Card No. 68-10888

ALL RIGHTS RESERVED
Published simultaneously in Canada by
George J. McLeod Limited, Toronto

Designed by Nancy H. Dale
PRINTED IN THE UNITED STATES OF AMERICA
1 2 3 4 5 6 7 8 9 0

PREFACE

CHINA: THE ROOTS OF MADNESS was conceived as a television documentary and presented to the American public in January 1967.

It is offered in this form both as a sample of the modern documentary technique and a short pictorial history of the Chinese Revolution. Where the imperatives of television time forced compression for final broadcast, several narrations of eyewitnesses were eliminated from the original study as composed in our studio. These have been restored in this volume. Otherwise, no changes have been made in the original script except for tense and grammatical changes, where the printed medium must impose its standards on the audiovisual standards of the original.

The writer and producer hope that the reader will bring to the words an imagination that can hear them as if spoken aloud, and as part of a whole in which the pictures bear as much of the message as the script.

Wolper Productions has provided the bibliography for those who wish to read more of China, and the short chronology of modern Chinese history. The brief biographies of Chinese personalities were edited by Donald W. Klein of the East Asian Institute, Columbia University.

THEODORE H. WHITE
MEL STUART

CONTENTS

Ours has been a century of blood and terror. And yet of all the convulsions of our time, the one we heeded least was the revolution in China, bloodiest and most terrible of all—an entire civilization blown apart.

There are seven hundred million Chinese today—one quarter of the human race. And they are taught to hate. Their growing power is the world's greatest threat to peace and life. Fifty years of torment bred madness. To deal with madness, we must understand its roots, see China's revolution through the eyes of those who were there.

For eighteen years, we of the West have been excluded from China. We can pace along the barbed-wire border at Hong Kong and try to squint inside or strain out sounds. But all we hear is echo of disaster, past and present.

When we ask why, there is no other book of answers but the history of this century. For both of us—Chinese and Westerners—have shared the blunders that transformed our greatest friend in Asia into our greatest enemy.

Interior view of Forbidden City, Peking. JOHN E. ALLEN

Theodore H. White narrating:

Those of us who lived in China remember it all so differently, so close they were in friendship to us, fingertip close. And now their fists are balled in anger. They were looking for some entry into the modern world, and nothing in their ancient culture could give them any guide to the turbulence they found.

Nor could we help them. It was a quest—a fifty-year search—for some new kind of government, some new form of order. And in the end, they moved from tyranny to tyranny; from the tyranny of Confucius and the Manchu Emperors to the tyranny of communism and Mao. In between, we've had only fitful glimpses of what happened, snatches of photography—tantalizingly incomplete—to explain what happened. It all began in mystery—and goes on today in mystery.

For two thousand years, we tried to read this Chinese mystery, but read it from a book of myths. Entrancing, age-old myths brought back by travelers from beyond the mountain walls of Asia where they had found a land of changeless wonders.

A strange serenity of spirit graced its hills with beauties, bridges arched across the rivers as much to soothe

JOHN E. ALLEN

the eye as help the wayfarer. The silent shriek of violence in art might catch attention, but that was echo of an anger we did not fathom. The same mythical serenity rested on all the fields of this land of peasants —a biblical rhythm carried men from sowing to harvest, from birth to death, in apparent contentment.

The old myth held that China had solved the great secret of government. Confucius—half god, half sage— had taught that order and duty make government, with each man fixed in place, bound in obedience to those above, as those above were bound in obedience to the Will of Heaven. They called the Emperor the Son of Heaven, *T'ien Tzu,* because only he interpreted the Will of Heaven in his land.

For fifteen hundred miles ran the Great Wall, sealing in a nation so proud it knew itself only as *Chung*

FOX

JOHN E. ALLEN

15

Kuo, the Central Kingdom. All other men were barbarians. For two thousands years, behind the wall, proud China knew herself invulnerable. For centuries, China let barbarian Westerners dock only at Canton to buy her precious silks, her porcelain, her tea. To pay for these, Englishmen introduced opium from India.

By 1830 this trade was booming. China protested—burned the opium—and the bark of English warships as war broke out in 1839 first shattered the myths of Chinese power. The result: defeat, disaster.

Aboard a British warship in 1842 came humiliation when China was forced by treaty to yield Hong Kong outright and open four more coastal cities to British merchants—and their opium.

Where Britain led others followed. Rival powers raced each other to carve proud China as spoils. English, French, Americans, Germans, Russians demanded privileges, colonies, concessions, and in sixty years had

Canton factories, *circa* 1815, from an old painting.

Opium smokers.

The Opium War. An English warship fires on a Chinese ship.

won the right to govern, try, and punish Chinese in their own land.

In China's capital, Peking, where from the ancient altars countless Emperors had sought the Mandate of Heaven, the myth of Heavenly Rule persisted still. But by 1900, deep within the palaces where China's Manchu Emperors reigned, that myth, too, was dead, for here ruled China's evil spirit: the Empress Dowager Tzu Hsi.

A Manchu concubine, bedmate to an Emperor for whom she had produced an heir, the Empress was a woman with a gift of malice; said to have poisoned her own son upon his throne; installed her infant nephew as Emperor; killed his mother; and then imprisoned him in 1898. She was an ignorant woman, but the unchallenged ruler of the Empire, her court a whispering of ladies-in-waiting and eunuch favorites.

Chief among them was eunuch Li Lien-ying, as depraved as she. When they were told that China needed

Empress Dowager Tzu-Hsi (*center*), with ladies-in-waiting.

Allied forces in China, about 1850.

大清國當今慈禧端佑康頤昭豫莊誠壽恭欽獻崇熙聖母皇太后

光緒癸卯年

◄ China's evil spirit: the Empress Dowager.
A detail of her hand. (*Above*)

Counsellors to the Empress.   LIBRARY OF CONGRESS

Flag of
the secret
brotherhood
known as the
Boxers.

ships to fight the foreigners, they used naval appropria-
tions—to build a marble pleasure boat in a nearby lake.

Only one conviction bound the Empress to her people: hatred of the contemptuous foreigner who tramped
her land. A thousand villages deep in China mirrored
her primitive hatred of the foreign devil.

Moreover, their passions found flag and leaders as a
secret brotherhood, the Boxers, began to flourish. Kill
the white man, burn his missions, said the Boxers, who
claimed that magic charms could make their bodies
impervious to Western bullets. With the Empress' consent, in early 1900, they began to kill.

One of America's great novelists, then a missionaries'
child, was, at the time, in China. Miss Pearl Buck recalls:

*The Empress Dowager had issued an edict that all
white people were to be killed; and many had been
killed, especially in the north, in Shantung, where men,
women, and children, missionaries and business people,
too, had been killed. But we were fortunate because we
lived in the Province of Kiangsi and we had a very good
viceroy; he was an intelligent man and he knew that it
was folly for the old Empress to think that she could*

A company of Boxers in Peking, 1900.

gain anything by killing missionaries and business peo-
ple because there would be terrible retribution. And so
he was so courageous as to insert a negative—a no, a
not—into the Imperial Edict so that it read we were not
to be killed. And that's what saved our lives.

Within the massive walls at Peking, for almost two
months, three thousand foreigners and Christian con-
verts gathered under siege to fight for life, their sandbagged embassies a bastion against Boxer fanatics.

From around the world, navies rushed troops to raise
the siege. Britons, Americans, Russians, French, Germans, and Japanese raced with field guns and modern
rifles whose bullets no Boxer magic could resist. Victory
was swift, punishment ruthless.

North to South, foreign forces patrolled the country.

The Chou-Yan Gate, Peking.

British legation sandbagged against Boxers.

Chinese dead at South Gate, Tientsin.

THE BOXER REBELLION

Europeans judging a Boxer.

Execution of Boxer leaders.

Polo-playing American soldiers in Peking.   BURTON HOLMES

Japanese soldiers began to explore China's wealth—
and covet more. In the shadow of Peking's mighty ramparts, American soldiers tasted war on Asia's mainland
for the first time and frolicked—China forever humbled.

Foreign diplomats and generals debated China's fate.
This land of endless villages crowding each other against
the skyline: was it really a nation, or only a geographi-
cal expression? The peasants: was their recent outburst
of passion madness—or something deeper? Their government smashed, still they toiled as they had for centuries in the three great river valleys falling from the
heights of Central Asia to shape their country.

In the north—Manchuria and the valley of the Yellow
River cradled one kind of Chinese, whose center was
Peking, the Manchu capital. There, dry northern wheat-
lands rolled over unknown treasure stores of minerals
which Russia and Japan both sought.

In the center was the valley of the mighty Yangtze

with its key cities—Shanghai, Nanking, Hankow, Chungking—where British and American power turned the
wheels of industry, oiled the way of commerce.

In the south—the third valley, the West River flowing
by Canton to empty at Hong Kong into the sea. In the
steaming southland, peasants stooped in paddies to
plant rice, and spoke a dialect no Peking Chinese could
faintly comprehend.

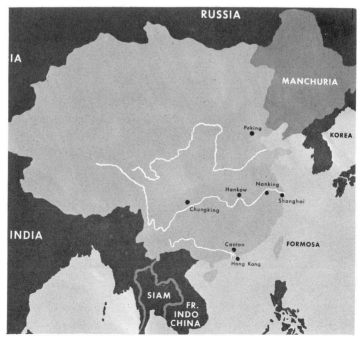

Human labor is used to pull a wagon.

The coastal cities, where most Westerners lived, squirmed with jostling people—animal energy. Humans were used as beasts in street and field. Most still wore the pigtail forced on them as a symbol of submission to the Manchu Dynasty and its Son of Heaven.

But within the Old Forbidden City, there *was* no government, no Son of Heaven. The aging Empress Dowager, her spirit broken by the Boxer War, lingered dying until 1908, after which, for all intents and purposes, the Peacock Throne was empty, save for a three-year-old infant installed to sit in it.

A crowded street in Canton.

The aging Empress, supported by courtiers.

White narrating:

And then it vanished. Simply vanished. The Manchu Dynasty disappeared overnight. Nothing like this has ever happened in all history. Two thousand years of tradition, the whole structure of the imperial Confucian political thought, dissolved in dust. The Chinese gave it a name and a date; they called it Shuang-Shih, double ten, the date being October 10, 1911, when a riot occurred in the Yangtze valley which could not be suppressed. Five weeks later, the regime had disappeared, the dynasty overthrown, never to reappear again in history.

Pearl Buck remembers this story about the Manchus:

They were butchered. You know, the Manchus were segregated in every city. It was a sort of luxury segregation—they were told that since they were the ruling class, they mustn't live like common people. But it was a Chinese device for administering the government, actually. To corrupt the ruling Manchus. That had gone on for a long time. I was in college then, but my mother wrote me that outside of our wall she saw—and I must say, she helped them—these pitiful Manchu ladies in their silks and satins, hiding in the bamboo

Yuan Shih-K'ai

groves and in the graves. But they were butchered.

Out of this turbulence there emerged two types of Asian leaders—arch-symbols—the men of guns and the men of ideas. These two types—the gunman and the dreamer—have perplexed all our efforts in Asia for the fifty years since, and they still perplex and haunt all our policy even today.

In Asian politics, gunmen rise first. General Yuan Shih-K'ai seized power at Peking and turned loose lesser generals to ransack the provinces. He gathered a puppet assembly, and imported an American professor to write a constitution for a republic. But the old ways were easier. Returning to Confucian order, in 1915 Yuan named himself Emperor—and six months later, died.

His rival, Sun Yat-sen, was the Man of Dreams. The dream of China—powerful, free of emperors and foreigners—made him, from his youth, a revolutionary. Students, teachers, and merchants meeting in secret headquarters joined his conspiracy. On postcards he scrawled a rising sun—the emblem of a new flag some day to be. For twenty years, he planned the destruction of the Manchu tyrants—only to see his dreams betrayed by Yuan Shih-K'ai.

A warlord army on the march.
◄ The Man of Dreams, Sun Yat-sen, and his wife, about 1915.

But Sun's ideas were catching fire. In 1919, students throbbing to his fiery message, sick of chaos, furious at foreign pillage, angered by Japan's demands for more of China, filled the streets with protest riots. But students had no guns, ideas no armies.

Armies belonged to warlord generals, the heirs of Yuan Shih-K'ai. Power and force were theirs, whether trained to fight with Manchu broadsword or equipped with second-hand artillery. Laughable to Europeans, in China such troops struck terror. Their purpose was simple—to rule by killing.

For fifteen years, a dozen regional overlords subdivided and morseled out provinces to lesser feudal warlords by the score. Warlord armies came in all shapes and weaponries—led by commanders colorful and grotesque: giant Chang Tsung-Chang, of legendary sexual appetite; Yen Hsi-shan, the treacherous drug addict; Wu Pei-fu, lover of flowers and gardens. Pearl Buck recalls:

They were a very practical sort of soldiers, those warlords. When they fought a battle, they would notify

us that they were going to have a battle the next day so we could stay home. And we had to watch because the shots would go right through windows. We had to sit in a corner of the room where you couldn't be hit and we learned to do that.

They never fought if it rained—they thought it was foolish to go out in the rain and fight. So if it were a rainy day, you were quite safe and comfortable and then, of course, they usually began at a certain time— they seldom began before ten, after everybody got a good breakfast and all that. They always took off for lunch and then by sunset, it didn't matter how hot the battle had been, when the sun set everything stopped and quieted down for the night so you could get a good night's sleep and be ready to fight the next day.

China watched such troops in shame, craving order, knowing sorrow.

Overlord in Manchuria was Chang Tso-Lin. Beginning life a common bandit, this scheming marshal had learned to mock all Chinese law, flout all patriot need. Bribed by Japanese industrialists, protected by their garrisons, his soldiers let the Japanese aliens exploit this northern treasure land at will.

(*Above, left to right*) Warlord commanders Chang Tsung-Chang; Yen Hsi-shan; and Wu Pei-fu. (*Right*) Chang Tso-Lin, overlord in Manchuria.

PATHÉ

Warlord Feng Yu-hsiang inspects troops.

Even the best of warlords, Feng Yu-hsiang, the Christian general—who baptized soldiers with a fire hose, insisting cleanliness was next to godliness—groped in vain to find a spark to unify his nation.

In every valley, town, and village, men trembled at the sight of warlord soldiers. Death came by twitch of trigger, in gusts of senseless cruelty. And life became so cheap that death itself became a spectacle. Children, growing up, became inured to violence; a culture of scholars was transformed by killing.

In flight from warlords, drought, and taxes, from loot and rapine, refugees knew that only in the colonies and concessions of hated foreigners could they seek safety. There, beggars for their bread, they might find mercy.

A former State Department officer, Ernest Price, remembers China in the midtwenties.

We hit the country at the time of terrific heat wave and, at the same time, drought in the great valleys. As our train pulled through this area, little boys at the stations would come—pot-bellied, spindly-legged, and holding out their hands and saying, "Please, master, please." We were horrified. We never had seen anything like it. Our legation official said, "Now, boys, I

Beheadings by warlord soldiers. "Death itself became a spectacle."

Refugees begged for bread, but life for foreigners went on, undisturbed.   BURTON HOLMES

want to tell you something. Don't let this get under your skin, this sort of thing. You're going to see an awful lot more of it in China."

But in the Western enclaves of the coast, life—for foreigners—went on unchanged. In Hong Kong the skyline walled from passing tourists the sight of Chinese anguish. Permanent expatriates returned each afternoon to homes of splendor where countless servants made for Master and his Missy-lady a sunlit way of life old China hands still mourn.

From Shanghai, foreigners controlled most Chinese industries—mines, mills, and railways. They set her tariffs, collected taxes. Prosperity rested as it always had on foreign guns and gunboats, within whose shelter Western pleasures, undisturbed, rolled on. At racecourses and resorts Chinese appeared, as always, as servants only; at Western clubs, the tinkle of ice in cocktails rose above the muffled sound of warlord guns outside.

Pearl Buck and her family came and went through Shanghai as a port:

It was a cold city to me. But there was everything that you could imagine in a city. Great wealth, both of

*Westerners—Americans and British and Europeans—
and Chinese, and all the retired warlords, when they
had gathered all the loot that they could from the people, would go into huge palaces there and take all their
concubines. I remember one old warlord who was famous because, he said, there were three things he didn't
know: he didn't know how many soldiers he had; he
didn't know how much money he had; and he didn't
know how many concubines he had. But he took all
that to Shanghai and lived a high life. Then there were
so many desperately poor there, too, because in famine
times it was there that the refugees went, and in cold
weather there were sort of wagons that went and
picked up stiff, frozen bodies from the streets. And no-
body seemed to care about anything. Everybody was
out for spending money and having a good time.*

Yet even in Shanghai, if one listened, one could
hear another note. In the streets, students were calling
for revolt. They were middle-class youngsters—yet their
message caught the ear of workers too. By 1925, fer-
ment had unsettled every major city.

The symbol of all protest was Sun Yat-sen, who
called on China to slay the dragon of imperialism.
Slowly through the early 1920s, Sun Yat-sen somehow

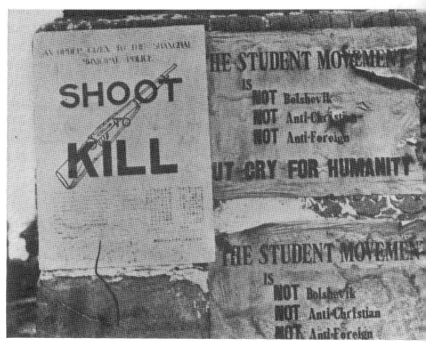

By 1925, students were calling for revolt.

built a government and won a tiny foothold at Canton,
ringed by hostile warlords. By 1924, the aging revolutionary had learned that ideas and guns must go together. The ideas he hammered into three principles
called *San Min Chu I*: first, nationalism; next democracy; then, socialism.

To his Nationalist Party, the Kuomintang, he now
insisted that to conquer China they must *fight* to throw
the warlords and imperialists out. They would get guns,
he promised, for he had found a way. Spurned by the
West, he told the *New York Times*, in 1923, "We have
lost hope of help from America, England, France . . .
the only country that shows any sign of helping us in
the South is the Soviet Government of Russia."

Flatly, the *Times* report concluded: "The prevailing
foreign estimate of Dr. Sun has been that he is a
dreamer and therefore dangerous."

Arch-symbol of Russian help was Michael Borodin, veteran agent of the Comintern, who brought the guidance of the Bolsheviks to Sun's dreaming. Counseling, scheming, urging, the mentor Communist became an all-pervasive influence, induced Sun Yat-sen to let the tiny Chinese Communist Party—four hundred thirty members—join Sun's Nationalists.

Professor Earl Swisher, now Director of Asian Studies at the University of Colorado, describes his experiences with Borodin:

In 1924, I was teaching in Ling-Nan University in Canton. We heard about Borodin's arrival as a representative of the Comintern, and about his close relationship as an advisor of Sun Yat-sen. Through some of the members of the faculty, we invited him to come to the campus for a meal and he fell into the habit of coming over rather regularly, eating with us and visiting with us. After some months of acquaintanceship, he brought a manuscript in English which he wanted us to correct. This was a draft constitution for the Kuomintang, which had been reorganized and brought to a national stature by Borodin over the last few months. The constitution was actually translated from the Russian constitution of the party—the Communist Party—and

◀ First plenary session of the Kuomintang.

Michael Borodin, "who brought the guidance of the Bolsheviks to Sun's dreaming."

translated into English by Borodin. We went over it and corrected it, without being too critical, but we produced a finished draft of this constitution. Borodin took it back, got the approval of Sun Yat-sen, and took it to the Congress of the Kuomintang. It was approved and translated into Russian for submission to Moscow. And it became the constitution of the Kuomintang.

English was the only common language between Borodin and Dr. Sun. And the English draft had to be approved because this was their only common language.The draft constitution was virtually a translation of the constitution of the Communist Party in Russia. This does not mean, of course, that it was Communist or Marxist. But the organization—the structure of the party—was identical to that of the Communist party in Russia.

Sun gathered new-style Chinese officers to fight for country, not for loot. Of these, his favorite was Chiang K'ai-shek. Sent hastily to Russia for training, Chiang soon returned to direct the Whampoa Military Academy at Canton where patriots were being trained by Russians to be the officers of armies that were to give the dream fresh muscle.

Some scholars say that at this point Sun recoiled

Dr. Sun Yat-sen and bodyguards. Standing directly behind Dr. Sun is Chiang K'ai-shek.

Cadets at Whampoa Military Academy, Canton.

from communism, prepared to break with Russia. But no one knows, for in March 1925 death cut across the revolution. Sun died of cancer. Mandarins, scholars, warlords, soldiers filed by his bier in homage. All claimed his message as their legacy, all scuffled for his mantle.

A year's turmoil thrust up the heir—Sun Yat-sen's soldier-favorite, Chiang K'ai-shek. At thirty-eight, he seized leadership at the Canton headquarters of the Kuomintang. This man was known to Westerners only as a fiery Nationalist and revolutionary.

As he mobilized troops under Sun's new flag, all China waited for him to strike against the warlords. July 9, 1926—*Pei Fa*—March North! Half a million warlord troops were marshaled against Chiang's slim divisions. A political earthquake tore the land, for Chiang's soldiers were of a different kind. Fighting for a cause and country, they stormed through villages and fields, victorious as much by spirit as by guns.

Accompanied by Borodin, a Russian staff, and their wives, Chiang's headquarters pushed north by train. A forward fan of young revolutionaries, Nationalists and Communist alike, preceded the troops, calling to arms the peasants and workers who surged to join the banners of the new day dawning. Among them, then unnoticed, was a Communist intellectual, Mao Tse-tung,

This train carried Chiang K'ai-shek and his staff north on their expedition against the warlords. (*Left to right*) Michael Borodin, Russian adviser to the Kuomintang; Kuoming-yu, head of KMT propaganda; Mrs. Borodin; Mrs. Liao Chung-ka; the first Mrs. Chiang K'ai-shek; General Galen, Russian military adviser; Chiang K'ai-shek and his young son.

then thirty-three, who directed scores of peasant agitators to summon fury for the revolution.

Mao Tse-tung, early in the revolutionary movement.

By fall they had taken Hankow, and the Nationalist revolution moved its capital there. Then, exultantly, they raided the British concession, burned down foreign buildings, tore down foreign flags.

The tide rolled on, from Hankow down the river. By April, Chiang K'ai-shek had reached Nanking—and then a pause. Chiang waited. . . .

Upriver in Hankow, left-wing leaders of the Kuomintang no longer trusted their army's leader at the front. Borodin urged them to get rid of Chiang K'ai-shek. In four short years, the Communists had grown to sixty thousand. They told the left-wing Nationalists that no revolution is complete until peasants own their land, workers their factories.

Nationalists, (*above*) raid British concession in Hankow. Less than a year later, Borodin (*below*) urges left-wing Nationalists "to get rid of Chiang K'ai-shek."

1927. Chiang addresses anti-communist followers.

White narrating:

Chiang disagreed. Scholars of Chinese history still debate with enormous fury exactly what happened next and why. But I think it's the classic revolutionary question. Who gets power? To whom the fruits of victory? No one knows what went on in Chiang K'ai-shek's mind, but I think one thing must have been clear to him. Either they were going to get him, or he was go-ing to get them. And he wasn't about to be dismissed the way Sun Yat-sen had been dismissed from power by warlords so often. It was a question of who would strike first and he struck first.

April 12, 1927, in Shanghai was the night of terror, as Chiang's troops rounded up and butchered hundreds of Communists—students, union leaders, anybody they suspected. And when the sun rose, Chiang was in com-plete control of all the lower Yangtze valley.

After that for months and months, through 1927, it became a great big bloody, boiling stew, as left-wing and right-wing fought and warlords got into the act, and Communists tried to stage uprisings. It all ended in tragedy because for so long this country torn apart had waited for a government to give it unity and dig-nity. It expected so much of this revolution and now found that revolutionaries can be butchers too.

This long, tormented quest for a new order was to end in squalor. It ended finally in December 1927 in Canton when, on orders from the Comintern, the Com-munists attempted to stage a massive uprising and seize that industrial city and the Kuomintang struck back with counterterror.

Professor Earl Swisher witnessed the event.

The weekend of December 13, 1927, I went across the city for a holiday with some friends in another compound. Sunday morning, December 13, we were awakened early by firing and shooting. After breakfast, I started back to the campus of my university across the city and, entering the Bund at the northern end, I immediately saw that the city had been taken over by a hostile force, that there were barricades in the streets and patrols moving around. The buildings, the shop fronts were all boarded up and closed, and it was evident that some major development had taken place. As I started down the Bund, trucks began to appear with nonuniformed forces—peasants and laborers waving red flags and distributing handbills out of the trucks. Troops appeared mounting the barricades and minor skirmishes with Nationalist troops were apparent. Further down the Bund, I saw peasant and labor forces breaking into the Central Bank of China and eventually setting it on fire. Picking up a handbill, I saw that this was an announcement of the takeover of the city by Communist forces and the announcement of the establishment of a Canton Soviet.

On the following day, from the island in the middle of the river, we saw forces moving down from the north, crossing the island below the campus and then moving up from the southern side into the suburbs of Canton. These proved to be Nationalist forces that had gone upriver with the Northern Expedition and were now returning and joining battle to recover the city of Canton from Communist takeover.

The Nationalist forces came in on Tuesday afternoon. There was fighting and burning of parts of the city during the night and then the mop-up came on Wednesday morning after the coup had lasted only about forty-eight hours.

Identification of Communists was a very simple matter. They had wrapped red kerchiefs around their necks to identify themselves as Communists, and when the coup collapsed these were hurriedly stripped off to remove the identification. But in the rather humid climate, the red scarves left marks on their necks. And so a Communist was anyone with a red neck. Destruction of Communists was a very simple process: rounding up anyone with a red stain on his neck and executing him.

It was officially announced that five thousand six hundred Communists were killed in the street fighting and in the takeover, and the whole structure of the Canton Soviet was destroyed. Within a few hours, the bodies were stacked up and carted away and the city was restored to the Nationalist government.

CANTON:

December, 1927. Five thousand, six hundred Communists were killed.

EARL SWISHER

Some thought communism in China was forever quenched. But Mao Tse-tung did not. He had escaped, and watched in hiding. He would return to fight another day.

In the cities of the Yangtze, children and teachers, businessmen and soldiers pulsed to Chiang's call. To the north, south, and east, warlords still surrounded him. But the winds of fortune favored his expansion.

A fresh new face entered Chiang's life—the beautiful Mei-ling Soong, sister of Madame Sun Yat-sen, American-trained Wellesley-educated. Chiang took her hand in marriage; she was to be a major shaping influence in all his future thinking.

By 1929, Chiang had built a majestic mausoleum for Sun Yat-sen at his new capital, Nanking, and Sun's body was brought there. Pearl Buck remembers that day.

Chiang K'ai-shek came in and roused great hopes in everyone. I remember the first time I ever saw him was at the funeral of Sun Yat-sen; four years after Sun Yat-sen died, his embalmed body was brought to Nanking to be buried in the great tomb on the mountain there. And it was the first time I saw Chiang face to face—a very striking man with very striking bold, black eyes. And he had a presence.

I think that he might have been a great first emperor if there had been a throne to sit upon. That was the tragedy—that the very structure of government was destroyed by the revolution, so that there wasn't a government and he had to begin that government from the bottom—and he didn't understand government. He was a soldier and he didn't know how to make a government. He had plenty of advisors, most of them young Ph.D.s from the United States, very impractical and idealistic, and they didn't know how to make a government.

And all the time, he had the Communists to fight and he also had the Japanese threatening. That was a very difficult situation. I'm never inclined to blame him.

To Western eyes, this soldier's rule seemed like the first firm government of China in many years. Chiang, too, was changing, for his wife, as much American in thought as Chinese, led him to see the United States as friend, a source of loans and help.

As new railways stretched their tracks across the country, the new Kuomintang order Chiang had brought began to offer comfort and luxuries to the cities he controlled. Industry boomed. Production soared. Engineers and young industrialists found for the first

Affluent Chinese dance in a Shanghai night club.   FOX

time that careers were being opened to modern talents. Universities flourished and paraded their graduates, full of hope. In cities, department stores began to offer the Chinese a taste of every modern ware.

Modern dress took subtle hold on Chinese fashion, while rich Chinese, in centers like Shanghai, began enjoying privileges until now saved for foreigners.

Not such froth, however, but the primordial appeal of Chinese nationalism was changing Asian politics. Even in Manchuria the call of patriotism twinged the conscience of warlord Chang Tso-lin, causing him to flout his Japanese protectors.

Traveling by rail in the summer of 1928, Chang Tso-lin met his death—a Japanese plot that blasted him to bits, punishing him for what they called his treachery. His son, young Marshal Chang Hsueh-liang, succeeded to power in Manchuria. This junior warlord knew that he must either serve Japan as a puppet or go with Nationalism. He chose Chiang.

In Japan, this switch set off alarm. Military men controlled Japan. They mobilized. They had to strike soon. They knew that if Chiang extended his power to vast Manchuria, if China's four hundred million peo-

The bombed train in which warlord Chang Tso-Lin was killed.

His son, the young marshal Chang Hsueh-liang (*below*), succeeded him.

ple unified, then they most certainly would lose the Asian mainland.

On September 18, 1931, an attack was begun which Marshal Chang Hsueh-liang's warlord soldiers could not stop—and Chiang K'ai-shek was powerless to help. Striking simultaneously at half a dozen different points, the soldiers of Japan seized towns and rails. By the spring of 1932, they held all Manchuria, and renamed it Manchoukuo; it was a puppet state at their command.

Rage swept China. Generals exhorted their troops to stand by for the counterblow, demanded a war of national resistance to Japan—immediately.

For Chiang, the problem pinched. His foot-soldier armies were stronger than old warlord armies, but they lacked tanks, had old artillery, were just beginning to understand the airplane. He knew they could not match the modern weapons of Japan.

Not only that—he led a nation still divided. The Communists, struck down for good in 1927, had somehow swelled, by 1932, to become a major force again.

White narrating:

It was as if a ghost had risen from the dead. When Mao had fled in 1927 with his thousand Communist zealots, he was already disgusted with Borodin and clumsy Russian doctrine. He felt the key to revolution in Asia lay in the peasants of the countryside, not the big-city proletariat. Eighty per cent of all China's peasants lived in bleak and filthy villages, treated like brutes, imprisoned by officials, landlords, and loan sharks. And Mao's idea was simple: turn the hidden peasant anger against the local gentry, the local rich, as well as the unknown foreigners. Let terror claim revenge by stealth and night, with pitchforks, guns, knives, grenades. Give guns to anger.

Out of this idea he created his black miracle—the doctrine of partisan warfare. Divide the land among the landless; rip out roads, bridges, railways, so that formal armies must slog on foot, dissolve in garrisons, bog down. Turn the countryside into a total environment of hate. Let women, children, everyone not be afraid to die.

It was political warfare raised to the nth degree. And by 1932, Mao controlled a good chunk of the two provinces of Hunan and Kiangsi, and claimed the loyalty of nine million people.

Chiang insisted he could not resist Japan unless he first crushed this enemy within. From 1930 to 1935, he

Bi-planes of Chiang's air force of the early 1930's.

drove his troops to fight. His narrow politics saw only
one solution: Force must root out Mao's ideas with
bayonets, with communism no compromise.

Year after year, the civil war went on as expedition
after expedition ground into failure in peasant ambus-
cade, guerrilla war.

An American newsreel of the early 1930s innocently
reported this nameless civil war:

*Troubled China turns of the enemy within her gates.
These bombing planes on the Nanking government get
ready to attack the rebel strongholds in Kiangsi. Còn-
tact! High over the mountains, Movietone flies with
the air force of President Chiang K'ai-shek. This is an
actual bombing raid and as we sight the first of the
rebel villages, we commence the attack. Chiang K'ai-
shek is making desperate efforts to unite the various
provinces of China, many of which are torn by internal
dissension. And if he can't do it one way, he tries another, including bombs. China, Far East, land of ancient culture, land of bloodshed, rebellion and war!*

By 1934, Chiang had forged a blockhouse ring
around Mao's Communists and, squeezing ever tighter,
felt certain they were trapped.

Communists in marching order.

White narrating:

Then one of the most amazing episodes in history took place. As Chiang squeezed, they oozed, dissolving into tiny bands; they oozed through his fingers. In October 1934 ninety thousand men and women set out; not just an army, but a government, an idea, carrying

all their records with them on little yo-yo sticks, on what they called the Long March. It's a six-thousand-mile trek they made from Kiangsi in Hunan south to Kweichow and up to the Kweichow Plateau, then up across the foothills of Tibet and then down again out of the mountains, down into Shensi, where in those dry and windswept hills they made their base.

Mao at Yenan.
FOX

Ninety thousand had set out; they arrived a year later, in October 1935, twenty thousand left, and there they were to dig in. There, calling peasants to their cause, they finally fended off Chiang's pursuit.

In 1936, however, Mao's line changed. He called for unity against Japan: rich and poor must stand together, an end to civil war! Nationalist, Communist, warlords all must stand as brothers against the alien threat. This new line appealed to millions, but not to Chiang K'ai-shek. He, his inner counsels, and his generals insisted that a final mop-up of the Communists must still go on, and now entrusted the task to "friendly" generals in the north.

Yet, mysteriously, this final mop-up stalled. The most important front against the Communists was held by soldiers of Manchuria who had been driven out by the Japanese. These homesick troops had little stomach for killing other Chinese and, led by young Marshal Chang Hsueh-liang, they itched to tackle the Japanese.

In December 1936, Chiang flew to see the Young Marshal in Sian, to flog him on to sterner effort. In Sian, however, the Communists had convinced the Young Marshal that civil war must stop.

White narrating:

Then there happened one of those episodes that sound as if they were written in a book of "make-believe." We have no photographs because no one invited a photographer to witness a kidnapping, which was what happened.

Chiang was in Sian to urge the Young Marshal to fight the Communists and on the night of December 11 he was sleeping in a villa outside of town when he was wakened by gunfire. The Young Marshal and his troops were shooting their way into his villa and trying to kidnap him. Chiang was in his nightshirt and bare feet. He slipped out the back way, tried to climb over the wall, fell. He hurt his back, he lost his false teeth, his feet were bleeding as he ran over the rocks. And the Young Marshal's soldiers caught him and brought him back.

It sounds mad, but that's the way China was. And it got even madder. Because when they brought him back, they invited the Communists down from North Shensi and on December 15 the Communists, the Young Marshal, and Chiang all sat down to talk. The Communists and the Young Marshal said to Chiang K'ai-shek, it's time to end the civil war; we must all unite against the Japanese or else. They could have killed him but they didn't.

Chiang K'ai-shek agreed. He would halt the civil war, and he would form a united front against the Japanese. So on Christmas day they gave him a plane and Chiang K'ai-shek and the Young Marshal flew down to Nanking to announce that the civil war was over. But Chiang had made no promises to the Young Marshal, so he imprisoned him immediately and kept him prisoner ever after, even to this day, in exile on Formosa.

Christmas, 1936. At Nanking, members of the government awaited their President's return. In pain, he hobbled from the plane. He announced to his government and the world that a popular front of Kuomintang and Communists would now, united under his command, turn to face the menace of Japan.

Japan's Imperial tradition had, however, one cardinal rule—always strike first.

By July 1937 the war was on. The Japanese sought total conquest, not just another chunk of territory. They blasted the heart of China in the Yangtze valley, with Shanghai the first city to take the shock. The Imperial Navy shelled Shanghai at point-blank range.

76

SHANGHAI: 1937

Refugees of the Japanese onslaught. Abandoned baby (*below*) cries amid the wreckage of the North Station.

Japanese shell Shanghai waterfront. The *USS Augusta* appears
at the right.   NATIONAL ARCHIVES

Japanese soldiers run through a city street.   FOX

It had been a century since Britain first blasted China open, a generation since the bloodshed of the Boxers. Babies had grown to manhood without a year of peace. For twenty-five years, China had lived with warlords, guns, and terror—but now it must drink deeper of the cup of bitterness.

November—Shanghai falls. December—Nanking is sacked and raped. Through the winter and spring of 1938, the Japanese pushed up the Yangtze, destroying the decade-long achievement of Chiang K'ai-shek, ravaging the cities on which all future hope of Nationalist China rested.

In the north, a different vision of tomorrow's China guided the Communists. In a village in a mountain gulch they made a capital—Yenan. Their headquarters had paper windows and furnishings of bamboo; their troops were called the Chinese Eighth Route Army. But the united front dissolved—Red generals ignored Chiang's orders.

◀ Shanghai falls. Japanese troops, with arms raised in a banzai, stand on a captured building.

Yenan, where a different vision guided the Communists.

◄ Chairman Mao. (*Right*) Chu Teh, Commander in Chief of the Red Army. (*Below*) Peasant women spinning at Yenan.

Their strategy made an independent war against Japan. In rear areas like Yenan, soldiers raised their food. Mao himself grew tobacco, and Chu Teh, the Red Army's commander in chief, hoed his own cabbage patch. Peasant women spun and sewed the cloth for uniforms, and fashioned straw sandals for the soldiers.

White narrating:

You would come in on Yenan from the air, over the rippling, billowing, yellow loess plain of North China. It all looked the same. The plane would come down and it would begin to wander its way through the gulches and the arroyos. And then you'd see, off on your

right, a beautiful old pagoda—one of those ringed pagodas which was the only landmark near Yenan. You would peel off and you'd come down—right down into a dry gulch, a dry riverbed, and there was the Yenan airfield. All around you, on the sides of this valley, were holes in the loess soil. These were the caves in which the Communists lived. An ambulance or a truck—because they had no jeeps—would bring you to the hostel where they took care of foreign visitors.

What do I remember of Yenan? I remember the yellow, and that desert-blue sky above it and that arid, dry air that was like wine. And I remember the sound of the bugles in the morning waking us up and also the sound of singing, because the Communists in those days were always singing. I remember the caravans coming in there, so strangely mixed with the few trucks they had.

Most of all, I remember the people. You would try to get interviews and the higher up you went, the more difficult it was to get an interview. But the more interesting. If you were dealing with a lowly general, you'd get the usual half-hour interview. If you dealt with somebody very important, you might get an hour or two. The lower in the hierarchy you went, the more busy they were, the more harassed they were.

I wanted to see Mao Tse-tung, and I waited, with the Communists telling me that they would arrange it. And one day they said, "Can you see the Chairman— or Chairman Mao tomorrow?" And I said, "What time?" And they said, "Seven o'clock in the morning, is that too early for you?" I said, "I will see him at five in the morning." "No, seven in the morning will do."

I felt we would have an early-morning interview before Mao went to work. I went at seven, and there he was in his cave. We began at seven and we went right on through until about half-past eight, when he paused and said, "Now, will you have breakfast with me?" And we had breakfast. When breakfast was over, I expected to be dismissed and he said, "And now, Mr. White, what else do you want to ask?" and we went on until noon or close to one o'clock. And he said, "Now let's have lunch."

And that was the experience of other people. If you could see Mao Tse-tung at all, which was enormously difficult, he wanted to talk to you in depth. The astounding thing was that the telephone never rang once, nor did anybody intrude. He had the most enormous leisure to think of policy—to think of long-range matters —of any man I have ever met at the head of a great operation.

The whole weight of Mao's personality would sink in very slowly. When you met him for the first time, the round face, his habit of stroking his chin, the serenity of his bearing, that shuffling, ambling, almost half-crouched, bearlike walk of his, gave you the impression of enormous gentility and gentleness and sober reflection. It was only after a while that you came to realize that this serenity was reflection of an enormous self-confidence. It was as if there were a book of Chinese history, or a book of Chinese politics, which only he could read. He had the self-confidence of a teacher explaining the world to ignorant people. And yet there was an opacity to all he said. He was lecturing; he wasn't communicating or responding as Chiang K'ai-shek did. One had no sense of the personality, of the tempers or the passions or the sorrows he had gone through. One had only the impression of an enormously forceful man. Forceful enough to speak quietly.

The mind of Mao Tse-tung saw warfare differently from other men. I remember him saying to me that Americans thought the Communists would lose. They saw the Communists in the hills of Yenan, walking around with straw sandals, a ragamuffin army. Mao said that any wise European who had seen George Wash-

Lin Piao.

*ington's people at Valley Forge would have said that
George Washington was going to lose. It's true, he said,
that the Japanese and Chiang K'ai-shek have electricity,
airplanes, tanks and we have nothing, but then, he said,
the British had all those things, and George Washington didn't have electricity. Yet George Washington won.*

*You suddenly realized with a start that Mao Tse-tung
was not really sure of when and in what century electricity was introduced. The structure of his knowledge
was totally different from the structure of Chiang K'ai-
shek's and ours.*

Mao's knowledge of Asian war, however, was un-
matchable. With his generals, he lifted the doctrine of
partisan warfare to new levels. Lin Piao directed K'ang-
Ta, a training school for guerrilla leaders. Chu Teh de-
ployed guerrilla bands hundreds of miles to Japan's
rear.

The people are the sea, said Mao Tse-tung, guerrillas
are like fish who swim in the sea.

Within a year such troops had gathered two hundred thousand peasant soldiers. The Japanese may have
seized cities, but the Eighth Route Army held all the
North China countryside about them.

In the Yangtze valley, however, all through the summer of 1938, fortress after fortress of Chiang K'ai-shek fell. The Japanese crunched on. By October, Chiang's last two citadels were doomed. First Canton, then, four days later, Hankow fell.

Killing prisoners, spreading horror where they went, the Japanese convinced themselves that sheer terror would now, at last, persuade the Nationalists to quit—that the war was won. But still their prey eluded them. From Hankow, Chiang had planned retreat. His government was to settle at Chungking, in China's deepest mountain fastness—Szechuan.

The Nationalists set out. Pack laborers salvaged from the burning cities what few machines they could. Students hauled away school libraries. Beyond the mountains lay the safety of the Szechuan basin, its only entry by the cleft the Yangtze cuts, a steeper climb, say Chinese poets, than the climb to heaven itself.

Retreat continued all through the winter—expression of a will to fight that no disaster had diminished. Up through the gorges they pulled or poled their boats until finally, in 1939, the rearmost echelon of the sad procession dragged through. Behind, they scorched a trackless belt of no man's land to guard these last interior strongholds from the Japanese.

Nationalist retreat to Chungking.

Boats were pulled or poled up the gorges.   PATHÉ

Chungking was now the wartime capital—a city of another age, almost unchanged in sight or smell or sound from Manchu China, and there, among those backward peasants, the government dug in.

Spurning all Japanese peace proposals, the Chinese braced themselves for certain havoc, and—in the spring of 1939—it came.

White narrating:

On the night of May 3, 1939, the Japanese sent twenty-seven bombing planes. They came in about dusk, in a line. It was the first mass bombing aimed at a civilian population in the history of the world. I remember those planes coming in and those bombs coming down. The town was built of bamboo and wood. And it burned and it burned and it screamed—you could hear the flames roaring. When the raid was over, that was the night of an eclipse of the moon. According to ancient Chinese tradition, the eclipse happens when the Dog of Heaven tries to gobble up the moon. They have to scare the dog off by beating on gongs. There were the peasants in Chungking, trapped. The Japanese were attacking from above, there were air-raid sirens, and yet they had to scare off the Dog of Heaven from eating up the moon. I remember the sound of their gongs in the night—beating and beating—and the sound of the

Chungking, "a city of another age."   UNIVERSAL

gongs mixing with the wailing and crying of the wounded and the terror-stricken. It was the first century and the twentieth century, all that grotesque mixture of past and future that you could find only in Chungking.

Day and night the bombs continued, yet Chiang persisted. Powerless to strike back, Chiang knew that only America could help; his diplomats in Washington sought aid. But he had other troubles, too.

White narrating:

It was about this time in 1941 at the height of the bombing that I had my first talk with Chiang K'ai-shek about the war against Japan and its strategy. At the end, almost as an afterthought, he said, "Remember, the Japanese are a disease of the skin, but the Communists are a disease of the heart." That seemed odd to me because at the time the Japanese were bombing the daylights out of both Chiang K'ai-shek and the Communists, both of whom were allied against the Japanese. But now, in retrospect, it seems a prophetic remark, almost a vision of an apocalypse to come.

◄ Japanese warplanes rain bombs on Chungking.
Mme. Chiang K'ai-shek (*below*) walking among the ruins.

Japanese attack Pearl Harbor.

Those whom the gods destroy, they first make mad. On December 7, 1941, madness seized the Japanese. Striking at Pearl Harbor, they hoped to force America's consent to their conquest of China.

Now China had a mighty ally. America's arms would soon be hers.

Geography destroyed this hope. Supplies must move across the ocean to India, and then be flown to China across the Japanese blockade. American pilots braved the topless Himalayas to fly the Hump and carry what they could, yet they averaged only a few thousand tons a month for the army of four million Chinese soldiers. Feeding an elephant with an eyedropper, an American veteran called it. Discouraged Chinese leaders said: our arsenals make only fifteen million bullets a month, just four per soldier—how can we fight?

Americans discovered there were other reasons for poor Chinese morale—graft in their armies; corrupt, incompetent generals; soldiers who were ill-shod, underfed, and sick.

Major General Frank Dorn recalls his training mission at the time:

A visiting American general from Washington asked me if he could see some Chinese troops marching on the road. So we drove out and the first thing we saw, of course, was that the majority—big majority—of the men had dogs of one kind or description, size, anything that they could have stolen along the way, on ropes, on leashes, on anything. And he smiled and said, "Here they are, the GI's the world over—they all love dogs." And I said, "Yes, they certainly love these." And he wanted to know what I meant by that. And I said, "Well, this is their rations. When they run out of rice and other food, the dogs go .... ook pot."

Each division had a certain area which you might call their "recruitment" area. And they would send their own division agents to shanghai recruits, replacements, conscripts.

They would usually march down the roads tied together with ropes—I've seen them myself—ropes around their necks from one man to the next man as they staggered down the road. They sometimes had to walk two or three or four hundred miles and they were not taken care of properly. Rarely did more than 20 per cent, and often as low as 10 per cent, arrive at the division area.

In the Chinese higher staff, there was corruption, but

General Joseph Stilwell with American and Chinese soldiers.

it was a type of corruption that most Americans would find difficult to understand and any Chinese would be ready to accept. And that is, the commanders felt that they had a right to take a cut out of the men's pay. They had a right to take a cut out of the men's rations. And then, say, the division commander, the regimental commanders have to have their cut—the battalion commanders, and by the time it got to company commanders, there wasn't too much to take. By the time it got to the Chinese GI, there was very little.

Commanding General for America was Joseph Stilwell. A soldier's soldier, his mission was to train a
Chinese army to strike back. In India, where he trained
thousands of Chinese flown back across the Hump,
Stilwell learned to know their true ability. But he grew
bitter at their government, which could not nourish
them. He felt that they could attack and win if they
were led by honest officers, and insisted that Chiang
reorganize his army to throw the incompetents out.

In Chungking, this pressure irritated the Generalis-
simo. He knew that victory was guaranteed by the efforts of his allies. His thoughts were on the aftermath
of victory, the final struggle for power yet to come.

A weariness of spirit seeped through his government.
Something faded. They wandered, alien, through the
anachronistic city of Chungking; the fronts were far
away; America's "Flying Tigers" guarded the skies.
Their background of big-city life cut them off from
direct involvement with the peasant people. Little
luxuries, little pleasures occupied too many minds too
long exhausted by the years of sacrifice.

Nonetheless, the prestige of Chiang's government
grew. Foreign diplomats courted Chiang's favor, paid
him homage. In 1943, at Cairo's wartime summit conference, he sat with Roosevelt and Churchill, accepted

The Cairo Conference.

as the equal of the great, consulted on the strategy of global war, assured of China's freedom, China's greatness in the postwar world.

From Yenan's tawny hills, the Communists watched all this and brooded. Unrecognized by foreign powers, they knew their strength was growing. They knew: not foreign aid, but peasant emotions, gave power.

White narrating:

It was three or four hours between Chungking and Yenan by air. But how can you measure the difference? They were entirely different worlds. Chungking had a Western elite which sat on an ancient peasant system.

And this governmental elite was very much like our own. It was cynical, it was gossipy, it was full of criticism. No action of the government went unwatched or uncriticized. Every dinner table bubbled with conversation and the latest whisper or rumor about somebody's secret sin or somebody's secret deal.

You came out of a place like Chungking into Yenan; the contrast made Yenan look glowing by comparison. These were ruddy, healthy, earthy folk. They seemed to have an almost aboriginal innocence. On Saturday night, you would be invited as a guest to the regular Saturday night dance at Communist Army headquarters where Chu Teh, the Commander in Chief of all the Red armies, and Yeh Chien-ying, the Chief of Staff of the Red armies, and Chou En-lai—all the mighty of Yenan except for Mao Tse-tung—would come to waltz around. There was a huge room like a shabby YMCA auditorium and the orchestra had a few Chinese string instruments and paper-covered combs and a few horns. It would go thump, thump, thump, thump, and they would waltz around, very ponderously and sedately. One could almost forget that this staff commanded an army of hundreds of thousands of guerrillas linked by radio from the mountains of Mongolia to the Pacific Ocean itself. And underneath their good cheer and *their cockiness was an arrogance that was absolutely unshakable.*

Mao, too, was hardening. Like Chiang, he thought beyond the war to what must follow. Twenty years of flight and fighting had toughened him to hardship; but his memory too, was scarred—by Chiang, by white men, Russians and Americans alike. His troops increased daily behind enemy lines. His self-assuredness froze to dogma. He had been right so often when others made mistakes that his truths became, for Communists, a holy script.

Colonel David Barrett, chief of the American military liaison team in Yenan, watched all this and recalls:

They emphasized that they had to give the troops political training because the political consciousness of the peasants who made up the Chinese Communist armies was very low. So, therefore, they said, we had to give them political training. I told them, in the United States Army we look with disfavor on political training. We think we should devote the whole time to military training. And they said, that is not the case in our army, because we consider military training and political training as equally important and one cannot be neglected for the other.

Chu Teh agreed with Mao that power is what comes out of a muzzle of a gun. But ideas, politics, must motivate the man behind the gun, a concept that the Nationalists only dimly grasped.

White narrating:

I remember one event which proved to me how powerful Communist motivation could be.

It happened three or four months after I got to China. I was then a young war correspondent attached to the Nationalist government troops. We crossed the Yellow River into Shansi, went along the front for a week or so, and then I thought it would be quite a lark to go beyond the lines into Japanese-occupied territory.

I went with a group of Chinese Nationalist guerrillas who were organizing resistance behind the Japanese lines. There was a young Nationalist lieutenant and two horsemen and myself, and we traveled behind the Japanese lines for two or three days. Then the Japanese flushed us.

We ran like mad, and they chased us all day. By the time we arrived in a mountain village at night, the horses were completely worn out, saddle-galled and their flanks heaving. We were as tired and just as scared, and we asked the villagers to give us water and fodder for our horses.

I heard the young Chinese official say, "We are of the Eighth Route Army." And I said to him, "Look, we're Nationalists, not Eighth Route Army guerrillas." And he said, "Shut up, if we tell them we're Nationalists, they won't feed our horses or water them."

It was the first sense I'd ever had of the political grip the Communists had acquired on the minds and hearts of the people in the occupied areas.

As war wore on, American aid increased, and Chiang was pleased. Reviewing the new divisions Stilwell had trained and equipped, Chiang hoarded these splendid forces—they would be useful later.

Stilwell violently objected. He wanted to use them against Japan—he had no interest in future civil war. Stilwell felt that unless Chiang purified his government, not only was he no help in the war but once the war was over, surely the Communists would win.

Their quarrel grew. A mission under Major General Patrick Hurley, an Oklahoma politician, flew from Washington to heal the nasty breach. Chiang saw this as more white man's arrogance, a meddling in the politics of China. No compromise was possible and Stilwell, relieved of command in 1944, was certain that American involvement in Asia would be long and tragic.

Japanese surrender aboard the *USS Missouri*.

The world rejoiced when, in 1945, the Japanese surrendered—the guns, all hoped, forever stilled.

To sign the document of surrender aboard the *Missouri*, the Allies—America, England, Russia—invited Japan's first victim, China. In their eyes, China's only spokesman was Chiang K'ai-shek, who sent Nationalist generals to represent his people. The Communists were absent. For the Chinese, this was but the curtain to an act; the climax was yet to come in a clash with the Communists.

White narrating:

However mighty and powerful Chiang K'ai-shek seemed in Washington or in Chungking, to the Communists he was simply a rival, a new kind of warlord whose measure they could take. Ten days after we dropped the bomb, I remember Mao Tse-tung making that speech about "who will share the victory in China?" He said, "To whom should the fruits of victory in the war of resistance belong?" And he answered, "It is very obvious. Take a peach tree, for example. When

General Patrick Hurley meets with Mao at Yenan. U.S. ARMY

the tree yields peaches, they are the fruits of victory. Who is entitled to pick the peaches? Ask, who planted and watered the tree. Chiang K'ai-shek, squatting on the mountain, did not carry a single bucket of water and yet he is now stretching out his arms from afar to pick the peaches. I, Chiang K'ai-shek, own these peaches, he says. I am the landlord, you are my serfs, and I won't allow you to pick any. We say, you never carried any water, so you have no right to pick the peaches. We, the people of the liberated areas, watered the tree day in day out, and have the most right to gather the fruit. Comrades, the victory of the war of resistance has been won by the people with bloodshed and sacrifice. It should be the victory of the people and it is to the people that the fruits of the war of resistance should go. As for Chiang K'ai-shek, he was passive in resisting Japan but active in anticommunism. He was a stumbling block. Now this stumbling block is coming forward to monopolize the fruits of victory. We will not tolerate this. This gives rise to struggle. Comrades, it is a most serious struggle."

To stop this dreadful prospect, General Patrick Hurley—then the ambassador to China—flew to Yenan.

He talked to Mao: the war is over, he said, let there

be peace. He suggested that Mao and Chiang divide the country politically, but unify both rival armies under a central government. America would underwrite the deal. Hurley put a plane at Mao's disposal so that Mao could explore the proposition in Chungking.

Thus Mao, his safety guaranteed by the Americans, took his first plane flight—to his first face-to-face contact with the Kuomintang since the killings and uprisings of 1927. Six weeks of negotiation produced apparent agreement.

But in the field, the race was on. All across China,

General Hurley and Mao arrive at Chungking, August, 1945.

At Chungking, Chiang K'ai-shek played host to Mao. The plans
that lurked behind their smiles deceived all Western eyes.   UPI

the broken Japanese must sign defeat, yield cities,
garrisons, and guns. But which Chinese would take the
guns and occupy the cities—Communist or Nationalist?

The Nationalists, with all the transport of America
at their disposal, emplaned their troops to seize the
cities of the Yangtze valley. This ease of movement
gave them a larger appetite—and they dispersed their
forces up from the Yangtze to seize the cities not only
of North China, but beyond—Manchuria with its vital
industry and rails.

Nor would the Communists sit still. Together, Mao
and Chu Teh, like Chiang, decided that the key lay
in Manchuria.

General George Marshall, with Chou En-lai at his left. PATHÉ

They chose Lin Piao as the field commander to make the dash. From Yenan and North China they would strike east and north, while Chiang was readying troops to move from Yangtze ports and airfields.

By foot and pack train, Lin Piao set out. The Russians had temporarily occupied Manchuria by the surrender terms with Japan. The Communists expected to get from the Russians surrendered Japanese equipment and guns—and hold the countryside before Chiang arrived.

The rumble of inevitable clash caused America to replace Hurley with General George Marshall. This architect of global victory was sent to save the peace for which so brilliantly he had labored.

At Chungking, received by Chiang K'ai-shek, Marshall groped for an American solution to the bitter revolutionary surges of a strange Asian nation torn by barbarisms a generation old. He invited a Communist delegation led by Chou En-lai, the chief Communist negotiator, to meet with Chiang K'ai-shek's spokesmen at his Chungking headquarters.

Marshall suggested, and they agreed to, an American answer for China's search for order: a federal government that would peacefully permit the two parties to govern provinces each now held politically; freedom of speech everywhere; and the resolution of disputes by talk, not guns.

In January 1946, both parties celebrated a truce with a handshake. No paper truce, however, could mend a nation ripped apart by fifty years of killing. Within two months, troops were on the move again, each side blaming the other. A hundred savage skirmishes flared to full-scale war.

Manchuria was the cockpit of the struggle—the industry Japan had built and left was the greatest prize in China. Chiang's American-equipped troops seized all the major cities—only to find a hollow triumph. The Russian occupiers had looted every factory before withdrawal. Ripped-out sockets showed where great machines once stood.

For Mao, the fighting in Manchuria was prelude to the climax of his theories—the day when guerrilla bands would group into formal armies and shove frontal combat at a weary enemy. He fought for more than safety now. His ambition sought to mold all China to his theories.

110

Looted factory in Manchuria.   PARAMOUNT

White narrating:

*I asked Mao Tse-tung what their policy was with re-
gard to freedom of the press, and he said they believed
in absolute freedom of the press and absolute freedom
of speech. It wasn't going to be like Chungking when
they won—everybody would have the right to say what-
ever he felt—there wouldn't be censorship the way
Chiang K'ai-shek had had in Chungking.*

*I said, "Do you really mean that?" And he said, "Of
course we mean it." And I said, "Do you mean that if
you come to power, anybody will be able to print anything he wants in a newspaper or publish any newspaper he wants?" And Mao Tse-tung said, "Of course,
except for enemies of the people."*

*Nor would he ever define, and I was too young to
ask him to define, what he meant by enemies of the
people. Obviously now it means anybody who disagrees
with him.*

In the summer of 1946, Chiang returned his government to Nanking and, once again, as seventeen years
before, reported victory for his cause at Sun Yat-sen's
mausoleum.

Chiang K'ai-shek at Sun Yat-sen's mausoleum, 1946.

Shanghai seemed to thrive.   HEARST

The fighting in the north was only distant thunder
in the Yangtze valley. American advisors urged Chiang
to seize this moment to win the hearts and make firm
the loyalties of his people by new reforms. Thus in
Nanking, Chiang convened a Congress to write a modern constitution, in one last try to govern China by
the order Sun Yat-sen had preached.

But the thrust of all his background was still military. His troops must win by force of arms, and with
American arms, he felt the Communists could be
crushed. His troops dug in to garrison rail junctions,
cities they had occupied. American advisors insisted
that such a static defense was a major error. They
said he was pinning down his best divisions where
Communist guerrillas would isolate them.

Queen city of Chiang's victorious China was Shanghai, restored at last to Chinese rule, with all foreigners'
concessions wiped out. While battle flared in the northern provinces, Shanghai seemed to thrive, even though
the long war's dislocation had filled the streets with
hungry refugees and homeless laborers who offered
muscle-energy for little more than rice to feed them.

Refugees in Shanghai. Muscle-energy in return for little rice. HEARST

With inflation, paper dollars had no meaning.

But after fifty years of suffering, such sights were almost normal.

What worried Shanghailanders most was their money. For slowly, then more swiftly, through 1946 and 1947, the cost of the distant civil war destroyed the value and the meaning of their paper dollars. Inflation ruined the vital middle class of all the cities, the one great source of Chiang's political support. Novelist Stephen Becker remembers the panic years:

The inflation was heart-breaking. When I got there in August of 1947, the exchange rate was sixty thousand yuan to one American dollar. And when I left in September of 1948, it was twenty million yuan to one. This was a great human tragedy, and it was also a political tragedy. The peasants could fall back on a barter economy and try to stay alive that way. The businessman could raise his prices from day to day. But people on relatively fixed incomes were just ruined. And those were the people that governments usually rely on for some stability and some support, and sometimes even enthusiasm. They were the policemen, the firemen, the army, the professors, civil servants generally, even the students, who have always been a political force in China. If a professor had been making the equivalent

"Peace, whispered the Communists to weary minds."   HEARST

of a hundred dollars American money when I got there, he would have been receiving six million yuan. If his salary had been tripled over the next year, because the government did make efforts to keep up with the inflation, he would have been receiving eighteen million yuan, but at that time it would have been worth ninety cents American. In the summer of 1948, my wife and I had a continental dinner at one of Shanghai's best hotels and the check came to two hundred fifty million yuan.

Who lost China to the Reds, ignorant men would some day ask. But in 1948, sorrow scrawled its signature clear: too many years of death and flight, too many dreams betrayed. In fifty years of barbarism, a gangrene of the spirit had set in, erasing pride and will and hope.

Peace, whispered the Communists to weary minds, Peace. An end of roaming. Now submit. Peace, they said; accept our mastery. And peace.

Land, they said, to landless peasants, to refugees. Join us, they promised, and the land will be divided. Their cadres slipped all through North China calling meetings to share out the landlords' fields—which soon they planned to snatch away again.

Mme. Chiang K'ai-shek with President Harry Truman.
◄ The Communists promise land division to the peasants.

In summer, 1948, Mao made his master move: assault by frontal armies in Manchuria! Guerrilla bands emerged from hiding and formed up in full divisions, equipped with captured tanks, artillery, and guns, Chiang's garrisons were isolated by ruptured railways and hostile peasants. In November 1948, Manchuria fell.

Panic began among the cut-off Nationalist garrisons in North China. They surrendered by scores, then thousands, then full divisions, the equipment America had given them falling to the Reds.

In November 1948, Madame Chiang K'ai-shek flew to America, her second homeland, to make a last appeal for further help. But Harry Truman had had enough. Reluctantly he told her: American involvement must end.

And now the Nationalists, pursued by wrath as they in years gone by had once pursued the Communists, gathered at Hsuchow, the last bastion guarding the access to the mighty Yangtze's valley. For two full months, Chiang's troops fought on. In January, cut off, they were forced to surrender. Half a million soldiers were lost—the Communists poured southward.

The evacuation of Nanking, 1949. A missionary (*right*) departs from Shanghai.   PATHÉ

His spirit heavy-burdened, Chiang resigned his leadership, hoping that other men might court the Communists for better terms.

On April first, the Nationalists sent emissaries to Peking to plead with Mao Tse-tung. But they had passed the point of no return. No mercy, said the Communists. The new Mandate of Heaven required all Nationalists to lay down arms within three weeks.

Three weeks later to the day, the Communists uncoiled to cross the Yangtze. Their first target was Nanking—the hallowed capital of the Kuomintang.

In that capital, the will to fight had turned to dust. No man would stand the ramparts. Abandoning their positions, troops trudged away as silent people stood and watched. Too many warring armies had passed this desolate way to make them want to fight for any faith or politics.

No mainland refuge now remained. The fleeing Nationalists embarked what troops they could to cross the ocean to the island of Formosa.

Shanghai heard the message clearly as foreign businessmen boarded up their shops: "Go now, go quickly, for communism marches. Take what you can—but flee."

In pell mell haste, the Western powers evacuated the city they had built, for good and bad alike must leave. The businessman, come for profit, as well as missionaries, come to heal, must say good-by as out of the Yangtze streamed the last of Western influence —and farewell to a century.

On May 27, 1949, down Shanghai's princely avenues, the pleasure boulevards of yesteryear, rolled the victorious Red Tide. In six more months, all China would submit—Red Star would be triumphant over the world's most ancient nation.

Silently, the crowds observed their newest conquerors.

The boarded-up Ford Agency in Shanghai. PARAMOUNT

In Peking, Red Guards march to honor Chairman Mao. UPI

Today, the marble altars of Peking still beseech the Will of Heaven, as always. Chinese still gather there to listen to the voices that interpret Heaven's Will. For eighteen years, Mao Tse-tung, alone, has tried to shape their thinking, has offered them his universal truths, a dogma as changeless as Confucius', to freeze their muffled discontent and end their quenchless modern turbulence.

The image shown his people has been that of a teacher—grandfather, benign. Yet all have learned that those who cannot read his lessons will be crushed. His aging mind still lusts for permanent strife; the theme he preaches to old and young alike is hate.

Chinese children chant: "We are small militiamen, fighting U.S. imperialism. Uncle, we must grow up quick to liberate Taiwan."

Taiwan, the object of their hate, is the place we call Formosa. This rocky island, ninety miles off the mainland, has many meanings. To statesmen, it is the last remaining redoubt of the Kuomintang, where Chiang K'ai-shek with American arms, has re-equipped an army, six hundred thousand strong . . . and dreams of

Chiang, with treasures of the Imperial Museum.

reconquest. But Chiang is pawn to American policy; he cannot move these troops or fuel them unless America lets him do so.

Now over eighty, Chiang K'ai-shek bespeaks for mainland China another threat. In his flight to Formosa, Chiang carried the ancient Imperial Museum of Peking, the treasures of eight hundred years of Chinese art— the symbol of another China, beauty past. It is this echo of the past that has bedeviled Mao, who seeks erasure of all past. Yet how Mao's struggle goes, we cannot tell.

White narrating:

At the American Consulate in Hong Kong, there are cascades, mountains, piles of translations that come in from the Chinese. These are sandy, gravelly, gritty little bits of information that are meaningless, because we don't know who does what to whom in Peking; we don't know how they think or how they make up their minds.

No matter how hard we study China, we cannot predict such a thing as the Great Leap Forward in 1958; we can't predict such a thing as the Red Guard purge of 1966. It is as if there were a struggle of sea monsters going on deep, deep beneath the surface of our vision

Behind the wall, students learn higher mathematics, but peasants still work as beasts of labor. CBC

and only these bubbles come to the surface to tell us that these are terrible struggles, but we don't know what they're struggling about.

Today, in total ignorance, we strain to know of China as once our ancestors strained to peer across the mysterious wall—not knowing myth from fact.

We know that industry grows—steel production swollen ten times to twelve million tons a year, light industry soaring. But what comfort it gives the people, we cannot judge. We know that beyond the Great Wall live people of dazzling historical ability. The forefathers of today's Chinese first invented paper, printing, books, gunpowder, the clock, the compass. In 1967, the Chinese lofted rockets. In 1965, they synthesized insulin. In 1964, they unlocked the atom's secrets.

From behind the wall rise boastful statistics. But we know that China's people hunger, have barely survived one of the worst famines in all history; that, driven by Communist cadres, peasants work in communes, today still beasts of labor as their fathers were.

Behind the wall, tyranny has tried to reach beyond the body—to the inner recesses of the soul. A song taught to children goes: "I woke at midnight and saw

Behind the wall, the aging leaders clash.

my little brother smiling. I asked him why he smiled. And he said, 'I dreamed of Chairman Mao.'"

The purpose of all learning in China has been to fathom what goes on in Chairman Mao's mind—this mind, all are told, holds all the truths that ever were or will be. Neither age, nor place, nor class has allowed escape from pounding, the chanting of Mao's litany in railroad stations, in stores, at work.

Even those who built the wall so long ago must be forgotten, they have been told—there is no history but Mao's.

The aging leaders who shared the hills of hiding forty years ago, trekked the Long March, withstood Japan, America, the Kuomintang, must now again pass judgment on their revolution. They writhe and split.

Behind the wall, they clash—they seek replacement for a chief whose triumphs make him think he is the Voice of Heaven, the universal sage.

The Chinese make bombs. In ten years' time, there will be more. The nightmare problem of our time shapes clear: to reach the minds of Mao's successors with reason before unreasoning bombs take up the dialogue.

打倒防修！ 打倒美帝国主义！

打倒缅甸反动派

美帝 U.S.A.

EASTFOTO

It does no good to mourn the past. We pass along a road of time which, always turning, never brings us back to the crossroads marked "again." Perhaps we should never have disturbed the slumbering civilization of China. Or else let it awake itself and reach for us. Perhaps China is too vast to be governed by mercy. Yet if the Chinese mind craves order, they must be brought to recognize they are the biggest factor in the world's disorder, and we must untangle the madness of their minds.

The most difficult task in the world is to reach the minds of men who hate you. We do not flinch from the immediate tasks: to guard our skies, defend our friends. We cannot flinch from tomorrow's task: to reach the mind of China. We race today to reach the moon; to reach that mind is a task of equal difficulty and far greater urgency.

In the material which follows, the chronology of modern Chinese history and the bibliography of suggested further reading have been prepared by Wolper Productions. Donald W. Klein of the East Asian Institute, Columbia University, has edited the biographical notes.

◄ Red Guards perform a skit: "Down with U.S. Imperialism."

1839–1842   Opium War—China defeated by Great Britain, resulting in the Treaty of Nanking. This Treaty cedes Hong Kong to the British and opens the ports of Canton, Amoy, Foochow, Ningpo, and Shanghai to foreign residence.

1843–1844   Additional treaties with England, France, and the United States establish "most-favored nation" treatment and extraterritoriality.

1850–1864   T'aip'ing Rebellion—peasant rebellion led by Hung Hsiu-ch'uan. Hung was against foreign domination and the Manchu Government. He also favored agrarian reforms.

1856–1858   Treaty of Tientsin—legalizing the importation of opium and further rights allowed to foreigners in China.

1866   Sun Yat-sen born in village of Tsui, near Canton.

1867   Manchus dispatch a mission to foreign capitals, headed by an American, Anson Burlingame. He receives promises of good faith toward China.

1880   Chinese diplomatic missions established in important foreign capitals.

1887   Chiang K'ai-shek born in Chekiang Province.

1893   Mao Tse-tung born in Hunan Province.

1894–1895	Sino-Japanese War lost by China. Japan receives Formosa and concessions in Manchuria in settlement.
1895	Sun Yat-sen flees China when his first attempt at revolution fails.
1898	One Hundred Days of Reform—Emperor Kuang Hsu orders wide reforms but they are overturned three months later by the Empress Dowager.
1899–1900	United States diplomatic notes advocating an Open Door policy in China.
1900	Boxer Rebellion—antiforeign Chinese groups attack Westerners. Foreign troops land in China to protect Western interests and the Empress Dowager flees Peking.
1904–1905	Russo-Japanese War—Russia loses and Japan gains control of the Liaotung Peninsula. The Russians also agree to evacuate Manchuria.
1908	Empress Dowager dies and a three-year-old boy, Hsuan T'ung, ascends the throne. A constitution is established, but in name only. The real power still resides with the monarch.
1911–1912	The Manchu Dynasty falls, the Emperor abdicates, and a republic is proclaimed with Sun Yat-sen as its Provisional President. Chiang

K'ai-shek returns from Japan.

Two months after taking office Sun Yat-sen re-signs and General Yuan Shih-K'ai, a former Manchu official, becomes President.

1912–1916 Political infighting between Sun and Yuan.

1914 World War I breaks out and China declares herself neutral. Japan seizes German holdings in Shantung Province.

1915 Twenty-One Demands—Japan places demands upon China which would have amounted to relinquishment of her sovereignty.

1916 Yuan Shih-K'ai fails in his attempt to reestab-lish the monarchy. He dies shortly thereafter.

1916–1928 Warlord period wherein various military ele-ments in China fight among themselves for control of the country and China has no effec-tive Central Government for twelve years.

1917 China declares war on Germany in the hope of regaining control over Shantung Province at the peace settlement.

1919 China is denied Shantung at the Versailles Conference.

May 4th Movement—this demonstration is the beginning of a resurgence of Chinese nationalism and progressivism.

1921   Chinese Communist Party founded.

1922   Chiang K'ai-shek joins Sun Yat-sen in Kwang-tung Province.

1923   Sun-Joffe Agreement—USSR pledges assistance to China. A joint statement is issued recognizing that communism and the Soviet system are incompatible with China's needs at this time. Michael Borodin, personal advisor to Sun Yat-sen and political advisor to the Kuomintang (Nationalist Party), arrives in China as a special emissary from the Comintern.
Chiang K'ai-shek heads a special political-military mission to Moscow.
Third Communist Party Congress authorizes cooperation between the Communists and the Kuomintang.

1924   First National Congress of the Kuomintang. Agreement is reached on admitting Communists to membership.

1925   Sun Yat-sen delivers several lectures elaborating the Three People's Principles (Nationalism, Democracy, and Livelihood or Socialism).

1925   Sun Yat-sen dies in Peking from cancer.

1926   Chiang K'ai-shek moves against the Chinese Communist Party and has its members barred

from top posts in the Nationalist Party.
Northern Expedition is launched by Chiang in
an attempt to unify China.

1927   Chiang K'ai-shek takes Shanghai and establishes
the Nationalist capital at Nanking.
Communists in Shanghai attack foreigners and
their property. Chiang K'ai-shek holds a mass
purge of the Communists. He also dismisses
Borodin.
Mao Tse-tung publishes his famous treatise
"Report on an Investigation of the Agrarian
Movement in Hunan." Mao states in this re-
port that the peasantry, not the urban elements,
will provide the main force to overthrow im-
perialism and capitalism in China.
First Chinese "Soviet" established in the Hai-
feng and Lufeng areas.
China severs diplomatic relations with the
USSR.

1928   The "Soviet" at Haifeng and Lufeng is crushed
by Chiang.

1929   Troop-disbandment conference called by
Chiang K'ai-shek. Chiang attempts to reduce
military forces of the warlords but in doing
so, many demobilized soldiers turn to banditry
and pillaging.

1930 China regains her tariff autonomy, a right taken from her during the nineteenth century.

1930–1935 Chiang K'ai-shek carries out five military campaigns against Communist strongholds in Kiangsi and Hunan. The first four end in defeat for the Nationalists. The fifth is successful and the Communists are routed.

1931 Mukden Incident—the Japanese Kwantung Army strikes at Mukden as a prelude to the establishment of Manchoukuo.
The first Chinese Soviet Republic is established with Mao Tse-tung as Chairman.
During 1931 a number of serious floods occur in China and this exacerbates the political and military situation.

1932 The Chinese Soviet Republic declares war on Japan and calls on other groups in China to do likewise.
Japanese puppet state of Manchoukuo is established in Manchuria.

1933 The Japanese move South and invade Jehol Province. Their advance continues to a position that will allow them to strike Peking and Tientsin.

1934 Chiang is successful in his fifth campaign

against the Communists, and the Long March begins. It is completed when Mao Tse-tung and twenty thousand survivors establish themselves at Yenan in Shensi Province during 1935.

1936   Chiang K'ai-shek is captured by troops of the "Young Marshal," Chang Hsueh-liang, at Sian. Chiang is released after promising to devote his efforts to fighting the Japanese and not the Communists.

1937   Creation of a United Front between the Nationalist and Communist parties.
Marco Polo Bridge incident near Peking which marks the official start of the Sino-Japanese War.
The Communists rename their army the Eighth Route Army and their guerrilla group in Central China the New Fourth Army.
The Japanese take Peking, Tientsin, Shanghai, and Nanking. Nationalists retreat inland.

1938   Nationalists lose Yangtze Valley, Hankow, and Canton. Chungking becomes their capital.
Wang Ching-wei establishes a puppet government in Nanking.

1941   New Fourth Route Army incident wherein the Nationalists and the Communists accuse each other of attacking first.

1941   The Japanese attack Pearl Harbor and Singapore.

1943   End of extraterritoriality for foreigners in China.

1945   World War II ends. Within two weeks following the Japanese surrender, Mao flies to Chungking for a meeting with Chiang.

1945–1946 General Marshall dispatched to China by President Truman in an attempt to maintain peace between the Communists and the Nationalists.

1946–1949 Full-scale civil war erupts between the Communists and the Nationalists. By 1949 the Communists have captured Peking, Nanking and Shanghai and are on the road to victory. The People's Republic of China is established on October 1, 1949, by Mao Tse-tung in Peking. Chiang retreats from Nanking to Canton and then to Chungking. He and the remainder of his Government flee to Formosa during December.

1950   On January 5, 1950, President Truman enunciates a "hands off" policy for the United States in the Chinese civil war.

CHIANG K'AI-SHEK
(October 31, 1887–)

CHIANG K'AI-SHEK, President of the Republic of China, is the son of an impoverished east China salt merchant. His military career began in his early twenties when he attended Chinese and Japanese military academies. While abroad he joined the predecessor of Sun Yat-sen's Nationalist Party, and when the Revolution began in 1911 he returned home to participate. During the next fifteen years Chiang was deeply involved in the revolutionary movement, becoming one of Sun Yat-sen's associates and helping him resist military and political threats from warlords and Yuan Shih-K'ai, who tried to restore the monarchy.

In 1923, after becoming Sun's Chief-of-staff, Chiang was sent to Moscow to study the Russian military establishment. The next year he became commandant of the famous Whampoa Military Academy, which was established to provide the basis for a modern national army. At this time The Nationalists, on Russian advice, were cooperating with the Chinese Communists. Thus, many Communists were either instructors or students at Whampoa.

After Sun's death in 1925, Chiang emerged as the most important Nationalist military leader, though he was still less important politically than some of Sun's former colleagues. Between 1925 and 1927 he gradually eliminated these rivals, building his own power structure within the Nationalist Party. In mid-1926 he became commander-in-chief of the National Revolutionary Army and launched the Northern Expedition, a massive military effort to defeat the warlords and unify China under Nationalist rule. By late 1927 southern, eastern, and central China were in Nationalist hands.

In the spring of 1927 Chiang attacked his Communist allies, splitting the Nationalist Party and establishing a separate Nationalist Government in Nanking. The Party was reunited in mid-1927 when the Nationalist faction in Wuhan also broke with the Communists. In early 1928 Chiang began the second phase of the Northern Expedition, and by June, Peking had been captured, symbolizing the unification of China. In October 1928 Chiang became Chairman of the National Government of China established in Nanking.

In the early 1930's, after Japan occupied Manchuria, Chiang insisted that the Japanese be appeased so Nationalist forces could concentrate on fighting the Communists and the remaining warlords. Most of the warlords were defeated, and the Communists, after a series of "extermination campaigns" during 1930–1934, were driven into the remote regions of northwest China. To restore China's sense of national unity and purpose and to combat the Communist influence, Chiang initiated the "New Life Movement" in 1934, but its effect was limited.

By 1935–36 there was great pressure on Chiang to abandon the war against the Communists and concentrate on the Japanese. This culminated in the Sian Incident of

December 1936 when one of Chiang's generals, Chang Hsueh-liang, had him arrested while he was on a visit to the northwestern city of Sian. Chiang agreed to cooperate in a "united front" with the Communists against the Japanese. Formal agreement was achieved in mid-1937, shortly after the Japanese invasion of China, with Chiang still recognized as China's top leader.

The Japanese advance was very rapid, and the Nationalist Government was soon forced to take refuge in Chungking. China was virtually powerless until 1941, when the United States entered the war. In 1942 the Allies made Chiang supreme commander of the Chinese theater (including Thailand and Indo-China), and U.S. Lt. General Joseph W. Stilwell became his chief-of-staff. During the rest of the war there was considerable disagreement between Chiang and the Allies both because of the corruption and inefficiency of Chiang's government and because he preferred to fight the Communists rather than the Japanese.

After the war, the United States sent General George C. Marshall on an abortive mission to arrange a settlement between the Nationalists and the Communists. Chiang made token efforts to broaden the governmental base by calling a National Assembly which adopted a new constitution in December 1946, but the Assembly, after electing Chiang President in March 1948, removed any check on his actions by granting him sweeping emergency powers.

By early 1946–47 full-scale civil war had broken out. Because of Nationalist feuding, poor organization, and overextension, the Communists gained control of Manchuria during 1948. Meanwhile the civil government in the rest of China had become increasingly corrupt, and inflation raged. Chiang, foreseeing the Nationalist defeat, retired from the Presidency in January 1949. During the following months the Communist armies swept southward, taking most of the mainland. In December Chiang fled to Taiwan where he resumed the Presidency of the Republic of China in March 1950. He has remained on Taiwan since, never publically disavowing his goal of returning to the mainland.

MAO TSE-TUNG
(December 26, 1893–)

BORN INTO A moderately prosperous peasant family in central China, Mao had a varied education that included both classical and "modern" studies. He was keenly aware of China's weaknesses and spent many of his younger years in search of a coherent ideology at a time of national political chaos. He finally settled on Marxism and was one of the founders of the Chinese Communist Party in 1921. Shortly after this, individual Communist Party members were admitted into the ranks of the Kuomintang, and Mao, like many other key Communists, held various posts in the Kuomintang. However, his allegiance was always firmly with the Communists, and as the Kuomintang-Communist alliance began to falter, he worked in the countryside as a political agitator.

When the Communists were expelled from the Kuomintang in 1927, Mao fled to the countryside and finally made his headquarters in a stronghold in Kiangsi Province. In the ensuing years, during which Chiang K'ai-shek attempted to dislodge the Communists in a series of "extermination" campaigns, Mao formulated the theories of guerrilla warfare which were to become a key part of Communist military tactics. In 1934 the concerted attacks of Chiang's armies forced the Communists to abandon their Kiangsi base and to search for a new and more secure headquarters. This 6,000-mile year-long trek—the historic Long March to the Yenan area in the remote northwest—took the lives of about 90 per cent of Mao's guerrilla units.

As Japanese encroachments became increasingly menacing in the mid-1930's, Mao and his colleagues called for an end to Nationalist harassments and a "united front" to resist Japan. This was brought about in 1936–37 when Chiang K'ai-shek agreed to cooperate with the Communists; this uneasy alliance lasted until the war ended in 1945. During the war years Mao's base in Yenan was strengthened, and his stature as a national leader was notably enhanced. In the immediate postwar period, Mao and Chiang engaged in desultory negotiations, but the real issues were decided in a civil war that ended with the Communist conquest in 1949.

Already the head of the Communist Party, Mao became in 1949 the titular head of the Chinese People's Republic, and during the winter of 1949–50 he journeyed to Moscow where he negotiated the Sino-Soviet Treaty of Alliance, which became the cornerstone of Chinese foreign policy for the next decade.

The accomplishments of the Peking regime were particularly notable during its first decade. However, the failures of the Great Leap Forward in the late 1950's—when Mao attempted to accelerate the pace of communization—severely strained the power and prestige of his government. In the mid-1960's Mao turned on a number of his long-time colleagues, most notably Liu Shao-ch'i, who were dropped from the hierarchy during the Great Proletarian Cultural Revolution. In spite of these difficulties, he has remained the master of the Communist movement since the mid-1930's.

EMPRESS DOWAGER TZU-HSI
(November 29, 1835–November 15, 1908)

BORN INTO THE family of a civil servant, she became a concubine to the emperor and upon his death in 1861 put her son on the throne. Within a few years, by politics and poison and in cooperation with eunuchs, she gradually acquired undisputed power in the Imperial Court. She is perhaps best known for her suppression of a reform movement in 1898 and, two years later, for her encouragement of a secret society known as the Boxers. The Boxer Rebellion, characterized by anti-foreign riots and the destruction of churches, culminated in the siege of the foreign legations in Peking. This proved disastrous for China and marked the beginning of the end of the Manchu Dynasty.

Tzu-Hsi spent her last years successfully thwarting the reform plans of the enlightened members of the Court. Her half-century of direct and indirect rule ended with her death in 1908, and within three years her heir, an infant, was swept from the throne in the Revolution of 1911.

YUAN SHIH-K'AI
(September 16, 1859–June 6, 1916)

A GENERAL AND GOVERNMENT official during the Manchu Dynasty, Yuan Shih-K'ai was a strong supporter of Empress Dowager Tzu-Hsi in her endless political maneuverings. He held many high posts in her government, acquitting himself well both as a politician and as an administrator. When the Revolution broke out in 1911, he fought to preserve the monarchy, but on its abdication he became Provisional President of China with the nominal support of Sun Yat-sen.

It soon became apparent that Yuan was no believer in democracy or republican government, and that he wished a return to the monarchy. Sun Yat-sen attempted to have him removed, but Yuan had obtained foreign backing for his government and was secure in Peking. In December 1915, he announced the reestablishment of the monarchy with himself as ruler.

Faced with this formal repudiation of the purposes of their revolution, many of Yuan's former supporters turned

146

against him. He was soon forced to give up his plans and was removed from all effective power. He died in 1916, the last great figure of the old order in China.

SUN YAT-SEN
(November 12, 1866–March 12, 1925)

SUN YAT-SEN, the "father" of the Chinese Republic and the prime ideologist of the Chinese Revolution, was born in 1866, the son of a converted Christian father. Educated in Honolulu and Hong Kong as a medical doctor, he was exposed to Liberal thought, and by the mid-1890's had become thoroughly involved with revolution. He figured conspicuously in the series of anti-Manchu plots initiated after China's defeat in the Sino-Japanese War. Barely escaping with his life, he spent years outside China (most notably in Japan and the United States) organizing support for revolutionary action and formulating the famed "Three Principles" which would become the ideological basis of the revolution: nationalism, democracy, and socialism.

After the success of the 1911 Revolution, Sun was made first Provisional President of China, but he soon had to step down to former Imperial Viceroy Yuan Shih-K'ai as a concession to strong conservative elements in the northern part of the country. Yuan failed to reestablish the monarchy, and after his death Sun again attempted to head the country but was barely able to remain in nominal control of parts of southern China. In 1923, the Soviet Union sent Michael Borodin and General Galen to Sun for the purpose of reorganizing and strengthening Sun's Kuomintang. Their work was effective, but the country remained split with one power structure in the north, another in the south.

Sun journeyed to Peking in 1925 to attempt to resolve differences and create a unified government for China, but he was already fatally ill and died of cancer shortly after his arrival.

MICHAEL BORODIN
(July 9, 1884–September 3, 1953)

An early russian revolutionary, Borodin was exiled in 1906 and went to the United States, where he lived until 1917. He then returned to the Soviet Union and became a top Communist political agent, traveling to Spain, Mexico, and the United States and elsewhere.

In 1923 the Soviet sent him, as adviser to Sun Yat-sen, to help strengthen the Kuomintang, thus beginning a period of Soviet cooperation and counsel. Borodin encouraged the admission of the Communist Chinese Party into the Kuomintang and helped establish the Whampoa Military Academy.

After the death of Sun Yat-sen in 1925 Borodin's influence

lessened. He accompanied Chiang K'ai-shek on the Northern Expedition to unify the nation, but by 1927 Chiang felt that Borodin and the rapidly growing Communist elements were too dangerous. He ordered a purge and execution of hundreds of Communists and had Borodin expelled from China.

Borodin disappeared from Soviet public life during the 1930's. His death was announced in 1953, but he may have died earlier in a Siberian prison camp.

FENG YU-HSIANG
(1882–September 5, 1948)

A SOLDIER IN THE MERCENARY armies of the Manchus, Feng Yu-hsiang converted to Christianity after the Revolution of 1911, thereby earning himself the nickname, the "Christian General." He constantly manipulated alliances, changing sides with an eye to augmenting his power. By 1924 he commanded a large private army and was being courted by the Soviet Union, which he visited in 1926.

Feng joined Chiang K'ai-shek's Kuomintang late in 1926, and had his entire force swear allegiance, but he always held back his forces until he could strike a blow that would benefit him rather than the Kuomintag. In 1929 he came out in opposition to Chiang and fought several battles against the Nationalists until the Young Marshal, Chang Hsueh-liang, forced him into virtual retirement in 1930.

Feng went to the United States in 1946, ostensibly to investigate irrigation and water conservation facilities. During the next two years, coinciding with the decline of Chiang K'ai-shek's political fortunes, Feng became increasingly critical of the Nationalists. En route home via the Soviet Union in 1948, he died in a mysterious shipboard fire in the Black Sea. Feng was survived by his widow, Li Te-ch'uan, who became Minister of Public Health when the Communist Government was established in Peking in 1949.

CHANG TSO-LIN
(1873–June 4, 1928)

CHANG TSO-LIN, the warlord who unified Manchuria and played a major role in its integration into China, came from humble origins. Born into a Manchurian peasant family and receiving no education, he began his career as a common soldier in the Sino-Japanese War of 1894–95 and then returned to southern Manchuria to establish a local defense corps which, during the Russo-Japanese War of 1904–5, harassed Russian troops. He strengthened this force until it controlled Mukden, an important Manchurian capital. After the 1911 Revolution, President Yuan Shih-K'ai made Chang one of the city's two garrison commanders. In 1916, after threatening rebellion against Yuan, he became a military governor in south Manchuria.

By 1919 Chang had extended his authority throughout Manchuria. He spent the next decade in a series of military adventures and shifting alliances to push his control into north China. When defeated he always withdrew temporarily to his Manchurian stronghold.

In 1924–25 Chang negotiated briefly with Sun Yat-sen, but no agreement resulted. By 1927 Sun's political heir, Chiang K'ai-shek, and his Nationalist armies began to push Chang out of north China. Chang retreated to Peking, where he tried unsuccessfully to become head of the Chinese state. Increasing pressure from the Nationalist armies and an ultimatum from the Japanese (who had been Chang's ally) to the effect that he withdraw peacefully or be refused reentry into Manchuria forced him to give up the plan. On June 4, 1929, en route back to Mukden, Chang was assassinated by the Japanese. His son, Chang Hsueh-liang, soon succeeded him.

CHANG HSUEH-LIANG
(1898–

CHANG HSUEH-LIANG, the eldest son of the famous Manchurian warlord, Chang Tso-Lin, became the dominant figure in Manchuria after his father's assassination in 1928. At that time he had had considerable military training, first in a Manchurian military academy and then in his father's army, where he held responsible posts during the warlord struggles in north China.

After his father's death, Chang's immediate problem was whether to ally with Japan or support Chiang K'ai-shek's newly formed National Government. Pressure from Japan delayed Chang's decision, but after learning that the Japanese were responsible for his father's death, he pledged Manchuria's allegiance to the National Government in December 1928.

Like his father, Chang was an agile politician. In 1930 he refused to support a warlord coalition against Chiang K'ai-shek in north China, and when the coalition failed as a result, he moved his own troops into north China, nominally in support of the National Government. Chiang K'ai-shek, not having the power to stop Chang, was forced to admit his supremacy in the north and made him a deputy commander-in-chief of China's national army. However, while in Peking, Chang lost control of events in Manchuria, where the Japanese prepared to intervene militarily. In September 1931 Japan's Kwantung Army occupied Manchuria. Chiang K'ai-shek ordered Chang to withdraw into north China. By obeying, Chang began his fall from power. In 1932 he left his military command to Chiang and went to Europe. On his return in early 1934 he became a deputy commander in north China, but the following year his troops were transferred to the northwest to suppress the Communists whose headquarters were located there.

Chang's troops opposed fighting their Communist countrymen while the Japanese occupied their Manchurian homeland. Thus, in June 1936, Chang met with Chou En-lai, a top Communist leader, and agreed to wage a common struggle against the Japanese. In the following months Chang tried to convince Chiang K'ai-shek to adopt the same policy, but Chiang, who found it convenient to pit the troops of a potential rival against those of the Communists, refused. Consequently, on December 12, 1936, after Chiang had arrived in the city of Sian to announce a new offensive against the Communists, Chang arrested him, demanding that he accept a "united front" between the Communists and Nationalists to fight the Japanese. Complicated negotiations followed, with Communist representatives participating. Chiang was released on Christmas Day, apparently after having agreed to the "united front." Chang then accompanied Chiang to Nanking, an error which led to his trial and imprisonment. He has been detained by Chiang ever since.

CHOU EN-LAI
(1898–

Born in shao-hsing, 200 miles southwest of Shanghai, Chou was an early revolutionary activist. After a period of study in Japan he returned home in 1919 to take part in student riots, and then spent the early 1920's as a student and political organizer in France.

After returning to China he became deputy political commissar of Chiang K'ai-shek's Whampoa Military Academy.

Already a leading figure in the Communist Party, he played a key role in an insurrection in Shanghai that helped pave the way for the arrival of the armies led by Chiang K'ai-shek. When Chiang turned on the Communists Chou turned to the underground and, in the years from 1927 to 1931, was deeply involved in an extended series of internal disputes within the Communist camp. He went to Mao Tse-tung's rural stronghold in 1931, and three years later made the Long March.

When Chiang K'ai-shek was kidnapped by dissident leaders in Sian in late 1936, Chou negotiated his release and an agreement for a "united front" against the Japanese. In the years after the outbreak of the Sino-Japanese War, Chou spent most of his time in Chungking, the Nationalist capital, as the chief Communist representative to the Nationalist Government. In the immediate postwar period he was the key figure in negotiations among the Nationalists, Communists, and Americans (the "Marshall Mission"). With the establishment of the Communist Government in 1949, Chou became Premier and Foreign Minister. Before relinquishing the latter post in 1958 to Marshal Ch'en Yi, he distinguished himself as an effective figure in foreign conferences, including the 1954 Geneva Conference and the Bandung Conference in the following year. Throughout a career that spans half a century, Chou has always remained near the pinnacle of Communist power. His political agility has been most recently demonstrated during the Cultural Revolution during which, apparently, he has acted as the chief compromiser between the warring factions.

LIN PIAO
(1907–

L IN PIAO, Communist China's Defense Minister and one of its foremost military figures, was born in Hupeh Province, the son of a textile factory owner. As a youth he attended the Whampoa Military Academy, then presided over by Chiang K'ai-shek. After the 1927 split between the Nationalists and the Communists, Lin took part in various revolts against Kuomintang authority and joined Mao Tse-tung in the Red mountain fortress at Chingkangshan. In 1934–35 Lin led a vanguard column of the famed Long Marchers, after which he became president of the "Anti-Japanese Military and Political Academy."

When war with Japan erupted in 1937 he led Communist units to a series of victories. However, because of illness and wounds, he was forced to spend several of the war years recuperating in the Soviet Union. After V-J Day, Lin was in charge of Communist forces in Manchuria, and from there swept southward in a series of battles that culminated in the collapse of the Nationalists.

Lin's recurring illnesses kept him out of public affairs in the early years of the "People's Republic," but he returned to an active political life in 1955, the year he was named to membership on the Party Politburo. Four years later he became Defense Minister and a key aide to Mao in reinforcing the Chinese Communist ideology throughout the country. In the early days of the Cultural Revolution (1966) he emerged as the heir apparent to Mao Tse-tung.

WORKS OF A GENERAL NATURE

Barnett, A. Doak. *China on the Eve of Communist Takeover.* New York: Frederick A. Praeger, 1963. An on-the-spot report by Professor Barnett of major events in China during 1947–1949.

Chow Tse-tsung. *The May Fourth Movement: Intellectual Revolution in Modern China.* 2 vols. Cambridge: Harvard University Press, 1960. The most thorough and detailed analysis of the May 4th Movement to date.

Clubb, O. Edmund. *Twentieth Century China.* New York: Columbia University Press, 1964. A survey of the political history of modern China by a veteran State Department officer who spent two decades in the Far East.

Cressey, George B. *Land of the 500 Million.* New York: McGraw-Hill, 1955. The most complete and up-to-date geography of China available.

Fairbank, John King. *The United States and China.* Rev. ed. Cambridge: Harvard University Press, 1958. This is a standard work on China and an excellent introduction for American readers.

Fairbank, John King, with Reischauer, Edwin O., and Craig. *East Asia, The Modern Transformation.* Boston: Houghton Mifflin Co., 1965. Also: Fairbank, John King, with Reischauer, Edwin O. *East Asia, The Great Tradition.* Boston: Houghton Mifflin Co., 1960. A two-volume series, a classic work illuminating two thousand years of Asian development.

Feis, Herbert. *The China Tangle: the American Effort in China from Pearl Harbor to the Marshall Mission.* Princeton: Princeton University Press, 1953. A standard reference on Sino-American relations during and shortly after World War II.

Fung Yu-lan. *A History of Chinese Philosophy,* trans. by Derk Bodde. 2 vols. Princeton: Princeton University Press, 1952–

53. A standard reference and the most comprehensive English text on the subject.

Griswold, A. Whitney. *The Far Eastern Policy of the United States.* New York: Harcourt, Brace and Co., 1938. A basic reference on American Far Eastern policy during the first third of the twentieth century.

Latourette, Kenneth Scott. *The Chinese, Their History and Culture.* 4th ed., thoroughly revised. New York: Macmillan, 1964. A standard text by a highly respected scholar.

Morse, Hosea Ballou. *The International Relations of the Chinese Empire.* 3 vols. London: Longmans, Green, 1910–18. This is the standard reference for China's foreign relations with the West from modern times to 1911.

North, Robert C. *Moscow and Chinese Communists.* Stanford: Stanford University Press, 1951. A history of the Chinese Communist movement. North pays special attention to Chinese Communist-Soviet relations.

Payne, Robert. *Mao Tse-tung, Ruler of Red China.* London: Secker and Warburg, 1950. A full-scale biography of Mao. Unfortunately, it is not documented.

Schram, Stuart. *Mao Tse-tung.* New York: Simon and Schuster, 1967. The outstanding and fully documented biography of Mao.

Sharman, Lyon. *Sun Yat-sen, His Life and Its Meaning.* New York: John Day, 1934. A standard biography of Sun using a number of Chinese-language sources.

Snow, Edgar. *Red Star over China.* Rev. ed. New York: Random House, 1944. An account of the Communist movement in China by the first Western journalist to visit Yenan and interview Communist leaders.

Sun Yat-sen. *San Min Chu I: The Three People's Principles,* trans. by F. W. Price, ed. by L. T. Chen. Shanghai: Commercial Press, 1929. This is the accepted translation of Dr. Sun's basic Nationalist Party doctrine.

Tan, Chester C. *The Boxer Catastrophe.* New York: Columbia University Press, 1955. A highly detailed and authoritative study of this anti-Western event.

Tsou, Tang. *America's Failure in China, 1941–1950.* Chicago: University of Chicago Press, 1963. Tsou believes that the United States has had basic inconsistencies in its Far East policies.

United States Department of State. *United States Relations with China.* Washington: 1949. (Department of State Publication 3573.) This is the famous China "White Paper." It is an extensive history of official American relations with China, especially during World War II and up to 1949. (This publication has been reissued as *The China White Paper*. Stanford: Stanford University Press, 1967. This copy is much more useful than the original as it contains an exhaustive index.)

White, Theodore H., and Jacoby, Annalee. *Thunder Out of China*. New York: William Sloane Associates, 1946. A first-hand report by journalists of the Nationalist Government's corruption and deterioration during the latter days of World War II.

WORKS OF A MORE SPECIFIC NATURE

Bodde, Derk. *China's Cultural Tradition: What and Whither?* New York: Holt, Rinehart, and Winston, 1947. Bodde introduces the reader to some of China's major controversial problems concerning her historical civilization.

Buck, John Lossing. *Land Utilization in China*. 3 vols. Nanking: University of Nanking, 1937. Reprint ed. of Vol. 1, New York: Council on Economic and Cultural Affairs, 1956. Buck has made the most comprehensive and extensive survey of China's modern agricultural economy to date.

Chiang, Siang-tseh. *The Nien Rebellion*. Seattle: University of Washington Press, 1954. History of a rebellion that racked North China from 1853 to 1868.

Ch'ien Tuan-sheng. *The Government and Politics of China*. Cambridge: Harvard University Press, 1950. This work spans two milleniums but emphasizes the modern period.

Dawson, Raymond, ed. *The Legacy of China*. Oxford: The Clarendon Press, 1964. Dawson has edited a series of highly readable papers that discuss the cultural achievements of traditional China.

Dennett, Tyler. *Americans in Eastern Asia*. New York: Macmillan, 1922; reprinted New York: Barnes and Noble, 1941. A standard reference work on official United States policies toward East Asia during the nineteenth century.

Dulles, Foster Rhea. *The Old China Trade*. Boston: Houghton Mifflin Co., 1930. A popular presentation of Sino-American trade relations prior to 1844.

Fei Hsiao-t'ung and Chang Chih-i. *Earthbound China*. Chicago: University of Chicago Press, 1945. A sociological analysis of three South China villages.

158

Feuerwerker, Albert. *China's Early Industrialization.* Cambridge: Harvard University Press, 1958. An analysis of the nineteenth-century economic order and China's attempts to introduce Western innovations.

Fleming, Peter. *The Siege at Peking.* New York: Harper, 1959. A popular account of the Boxer Uprising.

Houn, Franklin W. *Central Government of China, 1912–1928.* Madison: University of Wisconsin Press, 1957. A valuable study of the warlord period.

Hsü, Immanuel C. Y. *China's Entrance into the Family of Nations: The Diplomatic Phase, 1858–1880.* Cambridge: Harvard University Press, 1953. A compendium of information concerning the accomplishments of foreign missions in Peking and Chinese legations abroad.

Hughes, E. R. *The Invasion of China by the Western World.* New York: Macmillan, 1938. The author examines the impact of Western ideas upon China during the nineteenth and early twentieth centuries.

Isaacs, Harold Robert. *The Tragedy of the Chinese Revolution.* Rev. ed. Stanford: Stanford University Press, 1951. A classic work on the actions of the Comintern in China during the 1920's.

Israel, John. *Student Nationalism in China, 1927–1937.* Stanford: Stanford University Press, 1966. An account of how the Nationalist Government attempted to retain the loyalty and services of China's educated elite.

Johnson, Chalmers A. *Peasant Nationalism and Communist Power: The Emergence of Revolutionary China, 1937–1945.* Stanford: Stanford University Press, 1962. The author maintains that the Communists' rise to power in China is best understood as a nationalist movement.

Kuo, Pin-chia. *A Critical Study of the First Anglo-Chinese War.* Shanghai: Commercial Press, 1935. One of the standard references on the causes of the Opium War. It is based on Chinese sources.

Lang, Olga. *Chinese Family and Society.* New Haven: Yale University Press, 1946. An analytical and comprehensive survey of the traditional Chinese family system.

Lewis, Ida Belle. *The Education of Girls in China.* New York: Columbia University Teachers College, 1919. The author discusses the effects of modernization in education and how it changed the methods of educating girls in China.

Li Chien-nung. *The Political History of China, 1840–1928,* trans. by Teng-Ssu-yü and Jeremy Ingalls. Princeton: Van Nostrand

Co., Inc., 1956. A highly authoritative textbook written during 1948 for Chinese students.

Linebarger, Paul M. A., Djang Chu, and Burks, Ardath W. *Far Eastern Governments and Politics: China and Japan.* 2nd ed. Princeton: Van Nostrand Co., Inc., 1956. Chapters 6 and 7 are especially helpful.

Liu, F. F. *A Military History of Modern China, 1924–1949.* Princeton: Princeton University Press, 1956. An excellent survey of the Nationalist Army. The author used five languages in his research.

Mao Tse-tung. *Selected Works of Mao Tse-tung.* 4 vols. New York: International Publishers, 1954–56. An officially authorized English edition containing many of Mao's important writings.

Mao Tse-tung. *On Guerrilla Warfare,* trans. and with an intro. by Samuel B. Griffith. New York: Frederick A. Praeger, 1961. Mao's famous treatise concerning guerrilla warfare which has become a basic text for other guerrilla leaders.

Michael, Franz H., and Taylor, George E. *The Far East in the Modern World.* New York: Holt, Rinehart, and Winston, 1956. A standard reference.

Morse, Hosea Ballou. *The Trade and Administration of the Chinese Empire.* 3rd rev. ed. London: Longmans, Green, 1921. A useful reference for nineteenth-century China.

North, Robert C. *Kuomintang and Chinese Communist Elites.* Stanford: Stanford University Press, 1952. Career and background information on Nationalist and Communist leaders.

Purcell, Victor. *The Boxer Uprising.* New York and Cambridge: Cambridge University Press, 1963. This is an authoritative study dealing with the background of the Boxer Uprising.

Romanus, Charles F., and Sunderland, R. *Stilwell's Mission to China and Stilwell's Command Problems.* Washington: Department of the Army, 1953–56. The official military history of "Vinegar Joe" Stilwell's World War II service in China and his disagreements with Chiang K'ai-shek.

Sheridan, James E. *Chinese Warlord: The Career of Feng Yü-hsiang.* Stanford: Stanford University Press, 1966. A study of Feng Yü-hsiang, often characterized as China's "Christian General."

Spector, Stanley. *Li Hung-chang and the Huai Army, A Study in Nineteenth Century Regionalism.* Seattle: University of Washington Press, 1964. A well-documented work that provides great assistance in understanding Chinese regionalism.

Sun Yat-sen. *International Development of China.* London:

Hutchinson, 1928 (?). Sun's program for industrial development of China through Western investment.

Tawney, Richard Henry. *Land and Labor in China.* New York: Harcourt, Brace and Co., 1932. A classic evaluation of the general economic situation in China during the early years of the Nationalist Government.

Taylor, George E. *The Struggle for North China.* New York: Institute of Pacific Relations, 1940. A detailed examination of Japanese encroachment in North China from 1937 to 1940.

Wang Ching-chun. *Japan's Continental Adventure.* London: Allen and Unwin, 1940. A survey of Japanese aggression in China from 1931 through 1938.

Wang, Y. C. *Chinese Intellectuals and the West.* Chapel Hill: University of North Carolina Press, 1966. An analysis of Western- and Japanese-educated Chinese and their role in China.

Weber, Max. *The Religion of China,* trans. by Hans H. Gerth. Glencoe, Ill.: The Free Press, 1951. A sociologist's attempt to explain why capitalism did not develop in China.

Whiting, Allen S. *Soviet Policies in China, 1917–1924.* New York: Columbia University Press, 1954. An excellent study of the period.

Wright, Mary Clabaugh. *The Last Stand of Chinese Conservatism: The T'ung-chih Restoration, 1862–1874.* Stanford: Stanford University Press, 1957. A study of the vigorous but unsuccessful attempts to rehabilitate the Confucian ethic after the T'aip'ing Rebellion.

Wu Yung, *The Flight of an Empress.* London: Faber and Faber, 1937. This work is based on the diary of an official who accompanied the Empress Dowager on her flight from Peking during the Boxer Uprising.

Young, Arthur N. *China and the Helping Hand, 1937–1945.* Cambridge: Harvard University Press, 1963. The Financial Adviser to the Chinese National Government from 1929 to 1947 recounts the history of foreign aid to China and the extent to which it was used or misused.

Yu, George T. *Party Politics in Republican China: The Kuomintang 1912–1924.* Berkeley: University of California Press, 1966. The author analyzes the Kuomintang's origins and its development up to the time of the Soviet-style reorganization of the Party.